CHANGING YOUR SPOTS

Changing Your Spots

A Guide to Personal Change

Terry Wilson

Gower

Published by
Gower Publishing Limited
Gower House
Croft Road
Aldershot
Hampshire GU11 3HR
England

Gower
Old Post Road
Brookfield
Vermont 05036
USA

British Library Cataloguing in Publication Data
Wilson, Terry
  Changing your spots: a guide to personal change
  1. Change (Psychology)
  I. Title
  158.1

ISBN 0 566 07987 9

Typeset in 11/13pt Palatino by Action Typesetting Ltd, Gloucester and printed in Great Britain by MPG Books Ltd, Bodmin, Cornwall

Contents

Preface

Some years ago I was listening to a radio programme and the views of an expert on the subject of change. During the discussion the expert said that the only people to welcome change were babies with wet nappies. I found this statement intriguing and wondered about it long and hard. The implication is that all change is distressing and distasteful to people. But surely this is not the case. I know many people who have made fundamental changes to their lives and have gained great joy and satisfaction. They would describe their transition from one situation to another as a voyage of pleasure. On the other hand, I have known people who have had change forced upon them and had to struggle to survive and cope with the losses that they have had to assimilate. These two responses to change highlight one of the most fundamental issues to be understood when attempting to manage change. Reaction to change and the conditions that it creates can be totally different whether the change is selfimposed or imposed by others. A manager may choose to resign his job for a subsistence living in an isolated cottage on the Yorkshire Moors. To him this may be the most satisfying and worthwhile experience of his life. Another manager may be made redundant and forced by circumstances to adopt a similar lifestyle. She may regard this as abject failure and rejection and may never accept the changed circumstances.

Reaction to change is usually related to the initiation and control of the change. Where the initiation and control are in the hands of the person affected there is usually a positive attitude. Where the opposite applies there is usually a negative attitude.

This book is aimed specifically at people who are having to deal with change that others have initiated. Some of this change will be welcomed by individuals while others will be shocked and perhaps devastated.

Imagine that you have been a loyal employee of an organization for 25 years and are called into your manager's office and told that the organization no longer requires your services. What do you do? How do you even begin to think about it? When this happened to an ex-colleague of mine he went back to his office and experienced almost every emotion possible from resentment, anger, bewilderment, rejection and frustration to relief, satisfaction, happiness and excitement. After about an hour his emotions settled to a feeling of acceptance and he started to plan his new career. However, he had worked at the company for only two years and was 29 years old.

Another person I know was turned down for promotion and became hostile, aggressive and resentful. He found it impossible to accept the decision made by his managers that he was not suitable to lead a team of engineers because he did not have qualities that would motivate a team. He turned his anger and resentment inwards and became sulky and uncooperative. This behaviour led to a physical altercation with one of his colleagues which was not reported to management. He was rapidly becoming a candidate for dismissal from his job. He was saved from dismissal through attending a teambuilding workshop, on which he received some forceful and direct feedback from colleagues on his behaviour. In the emotionally charged atmosphere of the workshop the feedback had an effect and he agreed for his own good to change his behaviour.

Few of us can escape change. In today's fast moving world

change is affecting us all of the time, and most of the time we can easily cope with it. The environment that change creates can be likened to the sea. Much of the time the sea is calm with ripples or small waves breaking on the shore. The sand and pebbles on the shore are in harmony with the waves as they yield and flow in rhythm to the movement of the water. In the same way most people are able to yield and accommodate the ripples and small waves of change that affect them. In fact, change of this low magnitude is healthy as it provides movement and a change of emphasis in our lives. As with the sea, we sometimes grow bored of looking at water that has no movement, and is perfectly flat and calm. Most of us would probably pick up a pebble and toss it into the water to create some movement that we can observe and enjoy. But the sea also changes mood when it is whipped up by a storm and then it can damage and create havoc in its environment. Massive waves can sink ships, flood towns and injure people. In the same way profound change can create turbulent and unstable environments where people are forced to resort to the primitive instincts of fight and survive. If the magnitude of the change is not so great that they are immobilized then they learn to understand the change, control their emotions, reactions and behaviour and steer their lives to new priorities. They clear the debris of their past circumstances and build new directions and sometimes a new life.

The handling of personal change does not have to be unstructured. It can be systematically managed in the same way that one would manage the buying of a house or a car. However, there is one principal difference between managing change and events such as buying a house. The management of personal change often involves the management of deep personal emotions and associated stress brought on by a person being under threat or not in control of the events that are transforming them. This calls for insight, understanding and management of a different kind, and the management of oneself. This book has been written to give you this insight and understanding so that your transition is less arduous and stressful.

Maybe the leopard can never change its spots – but you don't have to be a leopard. With desire, commitment and personal belief you can change. It may not be easy but you can do it by working through the sections in this book and applying what you learn from that process. Good luck!

Terry Wilson

Acknowledgements

This is intended as a sequel to my earlier book *A Manual for Change*, published by Gower in 1994. *A Manual for Change* took a broad organizational view of change whereas this book focuses on the individual. The content is a reflection and aggregation of the experiences of the many people I have met and worked with in the past years. Some of these have been family, friends and colleagues but most are people I have worked with on consultancy assignments or those who have attended one of my workshops. In particular I would single out my friend and colleague Ron Knight. We spent many years working together and developing our thinking on this subject and he will no doubt recognize several of the ideas in Stage II. The theme common to most of these people is that they were being subjected to profound and sometimes disruptive change. In dealing with their situations, the ideas and concepts on which this book is based were developed, and without them the book could not have been written. To these people I am eternally grateful for enabling me to use their collective experiences to develop a programme for managing personal change that can be used by many others facing similar changes in their lives.

Also to be thanked are Malcolm Stern and the team at Gower Publishing for helping and advising on the style, structure and title of the book. Their fresh thoughts and new insights were especially useful. Over the years that it takes to develop the ideas and write a book of this kind, one subconsciously develops a mind set to the subject. This blocks new thinking and the adoption of different paradigms. Malcolm and the team helped me overcome this difficulty.

I am also grateful to the three people who at different times expertly typed the manuscript, Lesley Gill, Lynne Bruce and Joanne Wilson. It is reassuring and motivating for a writer to see scribbled pages transformed into neat legible text. All three did an expert job and gave me a boost when it was needed. They enabled the destination to be reached – how successfully is for you to decide.

Terry Wilson

Using this book

This book is for anyone who wants to learn about the management of personal change. You should work through it if you:

- are personally experiencing profound change
- expect to experience profound change
- wish to learn more about the management of personal change.

The three stages

The book has three stages.

Stage I   Understanding change

The purpose of Stage I is to help you to understand that experiencing change and living with its consequences are part of modern living. There is no way most of us can escape change no matter how much we might try. Furthermore some change can be so far-reaching that it alters your life forever. Consider the ex-miners of the Nottinghamshire coalfields who trained as sewing machine operators in textile and car upholstery factories when their pits were closed in the early 1990s. Those men who could contemplate doing such work (and many could not) had their working life transformed by the job change. At the other end of the social spectrum many names in the Lloyds insurance market lost their luxurious lifestyles when they had to honour their commitments to pay off the insurance debts incurred by Lloyds.

Although opportunity comes from adversity, you will not see these opportunities while still clinging to past circumstances. No matter how painful it may be to forget the past you must forget it since a new life cannot be built if the past is ever-present.

Stage II   Understanding yourself

To manage change successfully you must begin to understand yourself and in particular the effect that the change is having on you. Adverse change that is not within your control and that transforms your life can cause great pain and even physical and psychological trauma. Anger, depression and other emotions are present and have to be recognized and controlled. Accommodating the change and dealing with your feelings must be seen as a process that takes time, sometimes months or years. You have to work on yourself at the same time as working on your external environment. To work on yourself effectively you must get in touch with your feelings and then gradually begin to understand and control them. You must assess your attitude to the change and begin to develop an approach that will take you forward. Emotional and intellectual upheaval are characteristics of change which have to be managed to new positions. You can achieve this yourself but the support and guidance of other people is often of great benefit.

Stage III   Moving on

Stage III concentrates on strategies for going forward and building anew. After working through Stage II you should have a deeper understanding of the effects of the change on you and be ready to adopt new attitudes and new lifestyles. You may have to accept totally different paradigms, or ways of thinking, if you are to overcome the past and live a fulfilling life. 'Moving on' will help you to develop new perspectives by capitalizing on your strengths and building these into your new foundations. Stage III also offers the opportunity for you to support others who are struggling to manage change. By helping others you gain deeper insights into the whole process of change management, which is invaluable both to you and to others with whom you have contact.

Where do I start?

Where you start in the book depends upon your needs. You can read it from cover to cover like a textbook or a novel, or you can concentrate on the sections that are most appropriate to you and the circumstances that you are having to deal with. For example, have you just had massive change thrust upon you, or are you stressed and distressed by changes being forced on you by others? You may be planning new ventures and initiatives or you may wish to know more about the management of personal change. To start, turn to page xxiii which contains a summary of the 14 sections. Read the summaries and if necessary briefly scan the actual sections. Decide which part of the book you wish to concentrate on, Stage I Understanding change, Stage II Understanding yourself or Stage III Moving on.

Interact with the book

Each section of the book is based on practical ideas and concepts that will help you to manage your change successfully. You need to understand these ideas fully and apply them to your own change. To help you do so, you will find that the sections contain the following elements:

- Detailed explanations of the main concepts on which the section is based. Often diagrams are included to elaborate and give greater understanding.
- Case studies that show how individuals have handled aspects of their own change.
- Questionnaires to enable you to explore an idea in depth. They often contain a measurement or rating scale and this enables you to score yourself on a measure of the change concept.
- Exercises designed to give insights into aspects of change and how you are affected.
- A spot check at the end of each section. These checks are to capture your insights and learning at the end of each section so that you can use them in other stages of your change management.
- Action plans that enable you to adopt the ideas and messages in the sections and systematically plan to use them.

All of these elements ensure that you benefit from the concepts and ideas of the 14 sections. You can reflect, ponder and juggle them around in your mind or discuss and test them out with other people. Used in this way the book becomes a practical tool in the management of your change.

Gaining maximum benefit

Change can overturn or alter some of your deepest-held beliefs which may mean adopting new ways of thinking about yourself and how you live. This can be a profound and lengthy process with several stages. Therefore at the start of this process you need to understand or decide on several important issues.

Support
Will you be able to manage the change alone or do you need help from others? Most people depend heavily on others for guidance and support at some stage in their transition from one

situation to another. These may be family, friends, counsellors, colleagues, advisors and so on. You may already be involving other people in your process of change and should therefore show them this book and discuss it with them. Work out between you how to use the book. Alternatively the need for others to participate may not evolve until you have advanced some way into your change process. Other people can be involved at appropriate points.

Reflection

Remember that the movement from one set of circumstances to another does not occur immediately but is a trying, uncertain and often lengthy process. When faced with radical change few people immediately know what to do. The process of managing change therefore benefits from your reflecting on your situation and considering all of the options open to you. Do not make hurried decisions that you may later regret. The passage of time combined with your reflection and consideration of your circumstances is a healthy process from which new directions and decisions emerge. The uncertainty and the stress that it brings may cause unease or even distress but in the long run it is well worth it.

Your learning

At the end of each section is a spot check for you to complete which asks what you have learned. Consider this question carefully as your answers will provide some of the fundamental insights into yourself, your situation and the change process. When completing the spot check do not merely reiterate parts of the text but try to identify the fundamental truths of the section for you. To do this you will have to reflect upon the section, your present position and what you have written and decided. One or several points will frequently emerge which add meaning and give great understanding to the messages of the section. These points will be the foundations of your understanding and management of the change affecting you.

The first step

You must first describe the change confronting you and also what you expect to gain from working through this book. If you are reading the book to learn about the management of change and are not experiencing significant change yourself then the next section will be irrelevant and should be omitted.

My change

The first stage in the management of your change is to describe the change and how it is affecting you. This exercise will help in two ways. First, by thinking about your circumstances and writing them down you will be clearer about the change, how it will affect you and possible actions that you could take. Second, by describing your emotions you will begin to expose your true feelings, enabling you to consider the extent to which they are influencing your attitude and behaviour and allowing you to manage them more effectively.

Description of the change
Describe the change affecting you. List the main features and the possible consequences to you.

Feelings towards the change

Write down your feelings using words such as angry, confused, happy, sad, elated and so on. After each word write a brief description of why you feel the way you do.

Feelings	Description

My expectations

Now write down what you expect to gain from working through this book. This step is important as these initial thoughts will guide your thinking and attention as you complete the exercises. Do not be too concerned if you can only describe your expectations in vague terms. As you progress through the management of your change, expectations will become much clearer.

My expectations

Summary of the sections

Stage I   Understanding change

1   Change is inevitable

You live in an era of radical change. No matter how much you hanker for the past when life and work appeared more stable and solid you have to recognize that almost everything is changing – working patterns, family relationships, technology, standards of living, politics, the environment, medical science and so on. Nothing escapes change. Living in a modern technological society means living with change and the uncertainty that it brings. The pace of change is also quickening and there will be no respite; this is how life is for most of us.

2   Everybody experiences change

In this new era you have to recognize and accept that you will probably be subject to radical and distressing change several times in your lifetime. Old industries close down, new ones open up, individuals change their jobs more frequently and may have several careers in their lifetime, and family break-downs and divorce are commonplace. Remember that you are not a lone victim: most people have undergone and success-fully managed their life to a new position.

3 Change can alter your life

When you are affected by far-reaching change, whether it be losing your partner, being made redundant, changing your job or moving house, you have to accept that your life has changed and may never be the same again. It is unrealistic and unhealthy to imagine that your life will always be the same. Be prepared for times of success, good living and enjoyment, but realize also that circumstances may turn against you and life become a struggle. You must learn to cope with the ups and downs of life.

4 Out of adversity, opportunity

Every pronounced change in your life is a transition to new circumstances and a new way of living. The successful manage-ment of change involves discarding the debris of the old life and rising to the challenge of the new circumstances. This approach requires personal vision, faith and resilience to see the opportunities that are present, to develop them and build afresh. Some change may present a future that is bleak and barren but it is up to you to build a different and better life.

Stage II Understanding yourself

5 Feelings

Change brings with it strong personal emotions. Learn to understand and assess your feelings. Emotions are positive in that expressing them brings a sense of relief but they can lead you to act irrationally which you might not have done if a more balanced assessment had been made. To manage change successfully you must manage your emotions. You can learn not to act on impulse and wait until your feelings are under control before making crucial decisions. You must also learn how your emotions affect your behaviour.

6   Change and stress

A person undergoing radical change will inevitably suffer from anxiety and stress. The loss of control, uncertainty about the future, possible break up of relationships, a changed lifestyle, and loss of material possessions cause stress. The stress may be revealed in many different ways such as permanent tiredness, loss of sleep, lack of interest, low motivation, sweating and palpitations, ill health and so on. Stress is a part of change that few people can escape. You have to take action to either divert or reduce the stress so that a reasonably healthy lifestyle can be maintained.

7   Attitudes to change

Your attitude to change will significantly affect how you are able to handle it. You may immediately see yourself as a victim, unable to escape from the actions and conspiracies of others. Your view is that the change being imposed on you will have a predominantly negative effect on your life. On the other hand, your attitude to the change can be the opposite. You see great opportunities and challenge with the chance to enhance yourself and your position. Your attitude is positive and forward looking and you apply yourself with energy and dedication to implementing the change and seeking the benefits.

8   Anchors

In a rapidly changing situation you must identify some anchor points in your life on to which you can hold. For example, a man may lose his job but his anchor point of a comforting home and trusting family gives him stability and help to overcome the change. A woman may change her job and separate from her husband at the same time. Her anchor point is her religion which gives her strength and the desire to carry on and develop a new life and new relationships. Most people can identify anchor points that act as foundations in the transition to the new future.

9   Transition periods

When you experience rapid and fundamental change you cannot expect immediately to embrace your new circumstances and feel comfortable with them. It takes time to shed the old paradigms and adopt the new ones, to dump old and now redundant attitudes, feelings and behaviour and develop new ones. This process can last weeks, months or even years depending on the nature and extent of the change and your personality. Transition periods are usually times of excitement, uncertainty or depression depending on the effect that the change is having on you.

10   Resilience rebuilds itself

Fundamental change to your job, career, lifestyle or personal relationships can alter your emotional and psychological stability. If the change is rapid and far-reaching you may go into a state of shock which leaves you with lowered self-esteem, lack of confidence and a general vulnerability. You feel less able to withstand the pressures and tensions of your work and life. However, this vulnerable state will gradually recede as the change is accommodated. Adaptation to new conditions will take place with the resultant rebuilding of confidence and resilience.

Stage III   Moving on

11   New paradigms

One of the most difficult aspects of adapting to change is the abandonment of old paradigms, perceptions, ideas and beliefs. Paradigms, or ways of thinking, are the foundations of your life and some changes destroy these foundations. For example, a person with 10 years left before they retire is made redundant with little hope of finding another job. Their retirement plans to buy a house in France and live off their pension are no longer viable. The paradigm has to be destroyed and replaced by another that is less ambitious. This process is very difficult and painful.

12 Facing the future

In times of rapid change it is easy to lose all sense of personal direction and to be buffeted by circumstances. If you have to abandon your direction you must seek and adopt another to sustain your stability. You will need to review the various factors in your life, appraise how they will change and take decisions as to which ones to concentrate on. You can also develop both a short and longer term strategy for dealing with the change and implementing your new future. Important factors that will influence the implementation of the strategy must also be identified and managed.

13 Developing strength

You need strength, resilience and maturity to manage profound change successfully. Your strength will come from a number of sources. You must be aware of these sources, such as being in control, ability to deal with a crisis, achievements, clear goals, a balanced life and so on. Each of the sources must be explored in detail and assessed on its importance to your strength and resilience. The sources in which you are strong should be used in managing your change. Other less developed sources should be examined and plans made to make them stronger to increase your confidence and strength.

14 Helping others

Helping other people to manage their personal change will greatly assist you to understand change and your own reactions to it. As the adage states: 'You really learn a subject when you have to teach it.' Before you can be a successful teacher or coach you have to understand a subject in depth. This involves study and the thinking through of ideas and concepts. Furthermore your interaction with the learners will bring new perspectives which add to your understanding of the total change process and the steps that individuals must take to manage it successfully.

STAGE I
Understanding change

Introduction

Change is a strange phenomenon. Like the air that we breathe it is all around us and as with air the impact on us is huge. No air means instant death. Fresh air invigorates us. Polluted air results in human ailments and disease. So it is also with change. No change can lead to stagnation and decay. Too much change gives rise to turbulence and instability. Moderate change can produce interest and pleasure.

Most people learn about change by being on the receiving end of it. Something happens to them or their environment and they react. If the change brings with it pleasurable circumstances then the individual is happy. If the change brings the opposite, and despair is the result, then the individual seeks ways to curtail or minimize the distress and move to a position of stability. All individuals who experience change that is detrimental to themselves are looking for means of coping better. This process is greatly aided by understanding change and the effects that it has on you.

Stage I of this book is written to help you attain this deeper understanding of change to enable you to manage yourself through it more successfully.

1 Change is inevitable

There is nothing permanent except change.
Heraclitus

You must understand and accept that you will experience extreme change several times in your life. You may have to live with change as a way of life. Organizations are changing, work patterns and the content of work are changing and personal circumstances are changing. The reality of living that many people must accept is that they will undergo several changes of job or career, failed personal relationships and fluctuating personal circumstances. Stability is a thing of the past for most people. You cannot escape change.

In this section you will begin to understand some of the sources of change which are introducing new dimensions and practices into your life.

Understanding change

A simple way of understanding change is to look back at how things used to be. How far you can look back will of course depend on your age. A centenarian may remember the horse as the main mode of transport, household illumination by candlelight and gas-light, people who never travelled more than 20 miles from where they were born, birds, bats and insects were the only things that flew. A 50 year old will remember the first black and white television sets, the building of motorways, astronauts in space, people moving from council estates to owning property, the three car family and having a job for life. A 30 year old will remember the first video-recorders, the first personal computers, the introduction of robots into industry, couples travelling to Jamaica to get married, equal opportunities and women's rights, package holidays and the collapse of Soviet style communism.

Almost every aspect of human existence evolves at an ever-increasing rate. Almost nothing stays the same. You must accept this fact if you are ever going to cope with and manage change successfully.

There were seven times more divorces in the 1990s than in the 1960s.	By 2005, half of the workforce of Great Britain will be working part-time, on temporary contracts or self-employed.

In the 1970s fewer than 10% of women returned to work within a year of having a baby. In the 1990s this figure had risen to over 66%.	In the four years to 1994/95 the number of full and part-time students in England rose by 40% to 1.3m. By 1998/99 it is projected that there will be 1.4m. students.

The number of people aged 75 and over in Britain is likely to rise from 4m. in 1994 to 6.8m. in 2034.

In 1972 52% of men smoked cigarettes compared with 27% in 1996.	By 2016 it is expected that 36% of all households will consist of a single person living alone.

By the year 2020 less than 2% of the entire global workforce will still be engaged in factory work.	Death rates from heart disease in the UK fell by about half between 1972 and 1995 for men aged under 65.

In the 1990s a baby girl can expect to live to the age of 80 compared with 49 at the beginning of the century.	In 1965 *The Times* published a list of the biggest industrial companies. In 1995 only 32 of the top companies were still in the top 100.

Some examples of change.

Exercise 1.1   My view of change

This exercise is designed to give you a broader understanding of change based on your own experiences. The exercise sheet on the following page lists a number of categories such as shopping, holidays, education, the family, marriage, business and so on. Consider each of these items in turn and then briefly describe the ways in which they have changed over a period of time, say the past 10 years. Also identify what you think has caused the change and then describe the effects that the change has had on you.

Example

Factor	Describe the change	Cause of the change	Effects on me
Shopping	The move to out of town supermarkets with a wide variety of goods and the pedestrianization of town centres.	Growth of the motor car. Supermarkets more efficient than single shops. Transport congestion in towns.	Easier shopping. More variety at a cheaper price. Town centre shopping more pleasurable.

Factor	Describe the change	Cause of the change	Effects on me
Shopping			
Holidays			
Education			
The family			
Marriage			
Business			

Factor	Describe the change	Cause of the change	Effects on me
Jobs			
Housing			
Transport			
Politics			
Government			
Religion			

Your reactions

After analysing the change that has influenced so many facets of your life try to sum up your views and feelings about it with a short phrase – examples are suggested below:

- Change is painful and it causes constant disruption.
- Technological change is bringing massive advantages while social change is far too rapid.
- Change is giving people greater freedoms and a better standard of living.
- Change is so far-reaching and complex that many people are being left behind.
- Change is exciting, constantly supplying us with innovations and new ways of doing things.
- Change is creating two nations, those who work and those who are unemployed.
- Change is creating more opportunities for people than have ever before existed.
- Change has brought about the breakdown of religious values and family relationships.
- Change is something I could do without.
- I thrive on constant change.

Write your phrase in the box below.

My change phrase

As you work through the other sections keep reminding yourself of your change phrase as the attitudes and feelings expressed in it will be reflected in the way that you manage your change.

You may well modify or completely change your views on change after completing this book!

Spot check

Now that you have finished Section 1, identify and describe the three most important points you have learned about change that will be of use to you in the rest of the programme.

My learning
1
2
3

2 Everybody experiences change

Would that life were like the shadow cast by a wall or a tree,
but it is like the shadow of a bird in flight.
The Talmud

After completing the first section you will have begun to understand that you have to live your life in a state of continual change, it is part of modern times. Much of this change you easily cope with because you are able to control it and it has little impact on your life. Other change may be far more profound and startling and upset the values and foundations of your life. It is change of this dimension that you must be able to manage. It is far easier to manage if you realize that many people experience this form of change. You are not alone and should not feel so isolated.

In this section you will assess how frequently people around you have had to manage profound change, which will help you to deal with the change facing you.

Other people's change

When you undergo change you can feel isolated from other people. You can become so engrossin the process that you lose a wider perspective and allow the change to dominate your life. Sometimes the change may be the breakdown of previously stable relationships as in the case of a divorce or redundancy. Such change adds to the isolation as a central feature of your life has been diminished or removed. The same process could occur in a change that has a supposedly positive cause. You may change your job in a progressive career move, which entails moving to another part of the country. Again, old and stable relationships with friends and relatives may be lost.

It is the feeling that it is only happening to me, or I am the only one to suffer, that adds a negative and stressful element to the change. If you feel that you are more adversely affected by change than others you should complete the following exercise.

Exercise 2.1   Other people's change

Identify five people that you know – friends, relatives, family members, colleagues or acquaintances. Write their names in the five boxes provided on the exercise sheet. Consider each of these people in turn and write down the changes in their lives that they have had to deal with in the past few years. Rate the change that they have encountered on the following 3-point scale:

1 – High level change requiring a radical rethink and adjustments to their total life and lifestyle
2 – Medium level change requiring substantial adjustments to their life and lifestyle
3 – Low level change requiring minor adjustments to their life and lifestyle

In the last column of the exercise sheet, describe to the best of your knowledge how each person managed the change.

Example

Person	The change(s)	Rating 1, 2, 3	Change managed
Joseph Goddard a neighbour	Made redundant from a position as marketing manager with a building company at the age of 55.	Rating 2. Lost income, lost, car, wife not working. Future bleak; perhaps will not work again.	Concerned, had a lot to offer. Systematically searched for jobs through networking. Obtained job as administration manager in a colleague's business.

Person	The change(s)	Rating 1, 2, 3	Change managed
1			
2			
3			
4			
5			

You have now considered the change that has affected people you know. Consider each person in turn and identify the factors that aided the management of their change. Write these factors in the box below. Obviously you will not have all the details about every person but you should have sufficient information to draw general conclusions. The types of factors that you will be looking for are:

- Showed great personal strength to withstand the disruption and pressures of the change.
- Good supportive network of friends and colleagues who helped and gave advice.
- Realistically assessed their situation and slowly developed a new life for themselves.
- Relied upon their religious faith to overcome the adversity.
- Accepted the change without question and quickly moved to a new venture.
- Went on a long holiday and came back a different person.
- Supported by a personal counsellor.
- Had a clear view of what was required and then went ahead and did it.

Change aiding factors

My change

The final part of this section is to consider the change that is affecting you, and if possible to identify the factors that will aid your change. Do not be concerned if you cannot immediately think of factors as these often only emerge as you work through your change. Note down any factors in the box below.

My change aiding factors

Spot check

Now that you have finished Section 2, identify and describe the three most important points you have learned about change that will be useful to you in the rest of the programme.

My learning
1
2
3

3   Change can alter your life

Tomorrow may be the last day of today.
Terry Wilson

If you are studying change or experiencing change you must understand and come to terms with the fact that change can completely alter your life. It is this fact that many people find so difficult to accept. Most people seek a fairly stable, predictable and ordered life and we just want to get on with living. And, indeed, periods of our lives are lived in this mode. However, when rapid and profound change is thrust upon us we are often intellectually and emotionally unprepared to deal with it. This section aims to introduce you to the fact that at *any time* massive change can completely transform your life. The change when it comes should not surprise you. This is life, you have to live with it!

Different forms of change

Change can be classified according to its type and the effect that it has on you, as illustrated in Figure 3.1. Figure 3.1 shows on the horizontal axis that change can be classified as simple or profound. Simple change is an occurrence that temporarily affects you but does not have a far-reaching and long-lasting effect on your life. Such events are the winning of £5000, breaking a limb, or a child leaving the parental home. This level of change may require you to make some readjustments to your thinking and behaviour. Most people would be able to cope without too much difficulty and after a period of time easily integrate the changed circumstances into their lives.

effect on you	happy	move to new house	win the national lottery
	unhappy	cancel holiday	divorce partner
		simple	profound

type of change

Figure 3.1   Forms of change

Profound change is brought about by events that can drastically change your life or circumstances. For example, the death of a spouse, business bankruptcy, breakdown of a long-term relationship, emigration to a different country, winning £10m. in a lottery. This type of change can alter the beliefs, values, attitudes and foundations on which life has been built. You may have to rethink your life and rebuild to suit the new circumstances.

The vertical axis of Figure 3.1 shows the effect of change on you. Some change makes you happy. For example, getting married, moving to a new house, achieving job promotion and winning the national lottery should be happy events for most people. They will be excited and enthusiastic as they adjust to the circumstances and opportunities that the change has brought them.

The other effect of change is to make you unhappy. Such unhappiness usually results from events which you would not have chosen to happen. Generally you have lost control of a situation and the change is forced upon you. The degree of unhappiness will depend upon the scale of the event. Damaging your car and the subsequent use of public transport while it is repaired may bring some temporary unhappiness. Being forced to cancel a holiday may have a similar effect. This unhappiness will be minor compared to the distress that may be endured following the death of your spouse, loss of a job, serious illness or divorce from your partner.

To assess and understand the changes that have occurred to you in the past, complete the following exercise.

Exercise 3.1   Change that has affected me

Reflect on your life over the past few years and consider the significant events that have brought about change. You may have experienced only a few events in the past 15 years or you may have experienced many significant changes in the past three years. Identify several events and assess them as shown in the example.

Example

Change event	Type of change	Effect on you
	Simple Profound └────╳────┘	Unhappy Happy └────╳────┘
Redundancy in 1990 from my job as a training manager with a large hotel group. Worked for the group for 11 years.	The change was quite profound as I decided to become self-employed and therefore could not look forward to a regular salary. I also felt a loss of status with my friends and family.	At the time I was quite happy about the event as I was stagnating in my job and needed a a fresh challenge.

Change event	Type of change	Effect on you
1.	Simple Profound └─────────┘	Unhappy Happy └─────────┘
2.	Simple Profound └─────────┘	Unhappy Happy └─────────┘

Change event	Type of change	Effect on you
3.	Simple Profound	Unhappy Happy

My change

Refer to your description of the change affecting you that you wrote in the section on page xix of this book.

My change	Type of change	Effect on me
	Simple Profound	Unhappy Happy

Spot check

Now that you have finished Section 3, identify and describe the three most important points you have learned that will be useful to you in the rest of the programme.

My learning
1
2
3

4 Out of adversity, opportunity

Each problem has hidden in it an opportunity so powerful that it literally dwarfs the problem. The greatest success stories were created by people who recognised a problem and turned it into an opportunity.
Joseph Sugarman

People generally have the greatest difficulty in managing change that is acute and that makes them unhappy. Under these circumstances they see the foundations of their life torn apart. As this happens they may become depressed and lose all sense of balance and direction. However, no matter how depressing the situation may appear, there is always opportunity in adversity. The opportunity must be identified, developed and used.

Identifying opportunities

Here are a number of case studies of profound change. These studies show the adverse consequences of change and also the opportunities.

Timothy's case
Timothy left the local secondary school at the age of 15 and completed an apprenticeship as a plumber and central heating installer. He was a hardworking and diligent tradesman and

a respected member of his company's workforce. At 24 he married Gail and they had two children, Emma and Susan. Over the next 10 years the family prospered as a cohesive and happy unit. Timothy was promoted to contracts engineer, overseeing the installation of plumbing and heating services in building projects around the country. Gail, while looking after the household and raising two children, worked part-time from home designing and making curtains and home furnishings for friends and acquaintances. They moved house several times and spent much of their spare time improving and redecorating their properties. Life was comfortable and orderly.

Timothy was then made redundant because of recession in the building industry. Despite all his efforts he found it impossible to secure another job. The family wondered how they would survive and maintain their standard of living.

Adversities

- The main source of family income had been lost.
- Timothy felt a loss of status, and a loss of self-worth.
- With the redundancy the family lost its main mode of transport, the company car.
- Timothy became depressed as he moped around the house with nothing to do.
- Gail felt under great pressure as her part-time work became the main source of the family income.

Opportunities

After a short time of depression, anger and confusion the family accepted its situation and developed the opportunities that were available:

- Gail expanded her part-time furnishing business into a full-time occupation, opening a small production unit and a shop. Timothy looked after the shop and helped with the cutting of material and the hanging of curtains.
- Timothy let it be known to friends, acquaintances and ex-

colleagues that he was available as a tradesman for sub-contract plumbing and heating work.
- Timothy busied himself around the house doing all the jobs that he had neglected for so long.

Gail and Timothy have been working in this way for several years. Timothy's sub-contract work expanded and he is now self-employed. Gail's business is thriving. They are maintaining their standard of living. The two girls are close to completing their education with the older one in the final year of a university degree.

Peter's case

Peter was a senior manager in an international manufacturing organization. Several of its units in the United Kingdom were in need of massive investment in plant, equipment, new systems and technology to enable it to compete in a tough and increasingly competitive market. Peter was appointed project leader of a business unit to oversee the refurbishment, which entailed the development and installation of new machinery, modern production lines, new computer systems and the re-organization of the workforce. A complete culture change had to be planned, programmed and managed. A philosophy, vision, targets and outputs were agreed and the project started. New equipment was delivered and installed and commissioning began. However, the length of time required to get the equipment working correctly had been seriously underestimated. After many months of trials and modifications the output of the unit was well below target and senior management replaced Peter as project leader. He was found a position in a planning unit, having little control of staff or resources.

Adversities

- Peter was mentally and physically drained after months of long hours, intense stress and pressure.
- Peter regarded himself as a failure and so did the rest of the organization.

- If Peter had run the project successfully he would have been assured of a more senior job in the organization, thereby satisfying his ambition. Instead he had been pushed into a backwater and his career curtailed.
- Although he managed to hide his true feelings, Peter felt a broken and dejected man.

Opportunities

After several months working in his new role and discussing his position with family and colleagues, Peter slowly began to take a more balanced view. Many of the factors that had delayed the project had been beyond his control. The greatest difficulties had been caused by the equipment manufacturers who had supplied machinery that had not been fully tested. The extensive modifications required had meant delays. Peter saw opportunities and decided to develop them:

- The learning experience of the past few years had been enormous and he would never again make the same mistakes.
- He realized his career within the organization was finished after 20 years of loyalty, dedication and hard work. He must therefore leave.
- He obtained a position with a consulting organization and eventually set up his own consultancy business.

Peter was very successful as a consultant and enjoyed a more fulfilling and prosperous life than previously.

Laura's case

Laura married Stuart when she was 17 and he was 21. At 28 she had two children and an unhappy and tempestuous relationship with her husband. Stuart was a bricklayer who was prone to bouts of drinking, rage and violence. After one particularly catastrophic weekend of rows and arguments Stuart packed a bag and left home, severing the relationship with Laura and leaving her to bring up their two children on her own.

Adversities

- Laura's immediate reaction was one of despair, wondering how she could possibly run a household and bring up two children with no money. However, her despair quickly changed to relief when she realized that the man who had dominated her life for over half her marriage and made her so unhappy had finally given her freedom.
- Laura wondered how the children would react to the loss of their father and whether this would create behavioural or attitude problems in the future.
- Although she realized it was not her fault, Laura felt some guilt that the relationship had finally ended. At times she reflected on the early years of her marriage when Stuart had been a much happier and relaxed person. Had she contributed in any way to Stuart's changed behaviour?

Opportunities

Laura's first priorities were to survive and keep the family unit secure:

- She sought and obtained maintenance from Stuart.
- She built up a network of friends and childminders in whom she could confide and seek help.
- She became closer to her parents and brothers and sisters.
- She started a part-time job with a playgroup to earn extra income.

With the children secure and her life reasonably stable Laura embarked on a pathway of personal growth and achievement:

- She studied to enable her to enter higher education.
- She gained a social science degree.
- She met Ralph who became a long-term partner and confidant.
- Her children stayed with her, left school and are in gainful employment.

Laura is now employed in a full-time responsible position. She has an absorbing relationship with her partner Ralph and is making plans for her retirement in 10 years.

Learning from the case studies

The three case studies demonstrate that opportunity does come from adversity. It may be a part of life that you must experience pain and unhappiness before you can discover new directions. The pain is the natural mechanism for breaking emotional ties with the past and thereby allowing new feelings and relationships to develop.

The case studies also show that the transition from one state to another takes time, very often months or years. You have to develop coping mechanisms to support you during the frustrating and stressful change period.

Exercise 4.1   My change

Consider the change that is affecting you and, using the exercise sheet below, analyse the adversities and opportunities as shown in the case studies.

Adversities

Opportunities

The last part of the exercise is to write an outline plan that will help you to manage and keep under control your adversities while exploiting your opportunities. Write this plan below.

My plan

Spot check

Now that you have completed Section 4, identify and describe the three most important points you have learned that will help you to better manage change.

My learning
1
2
3

Summary

Massive change is with us constantly, shaping our lives and our opportunities. Unless we wish to opt out, retire or become a hermit there is little we can do to avoid change.

Sometimes change is profound and transforms our core values and everyday existence. Overnight a lifetime's achievements and expectations may be lost. We may be required to adopt and establish a new set of beliefs and a different lifestyle. The loss of previously held values and material possessions can be extremely difficult to contemplate and adapt to. However, opportunity results from adversity and many people do better and achieve more from crisis and despair than they ever could have imagined.

Have faith and be convinced that your change will bring many positive benefits and lead you to greater fulfilment.

STAGE II
Understanding yourself

Introduction
Summary

Introduction

The most significant effect of change is the effect that it has on you. In the initial stages this effect is emotional and personal to you. These emotions can be so intense that they prevent you from operating effectively and may lead to stress and even despair. However, eventually you are able to understand and control your feelings and begin to manage them.

The management of your feelings and yourself is an active process which you have to engage in positively and work at. You have to explore your feelings and attitude to the change and try to understand why you feel, think and behave in the way that you do.

Eventually confusion and doubt are replaced by more positive responses as you build a new stable base and set timescales to achieve your new goals.

This understanding of yourself and your reaction to the change also leads to greater levels of self-belief and confidence to face the challenges of your new life.

5 Feelings

Every new adjustment is a crisis in self-esteem.
Eric Hoffer

Your feelings play an important part in the way that you perceive and handle change. If you are suddenly faced with rapid and extreme change you will first register it emotionally. You may explode with rage or you may remain cool and collected or you may become fretful. To understand and cope with change you must learn about feelings and the way in which they determine your behaviour.

Three parts of the person

To begin to understand how your feelings and emotions influence your reaction to change, study Figure 5.1.

This model shows the three main components to your functioning. You work intellectually, thinking ideas through in a rational and logical manner. You have feelings about issues and incidents in your life. And finally you take action. You will operate in all three modes. The significance of the intellectual and emotional components is that they both influence the action that you take. For example, two people inspect the

43

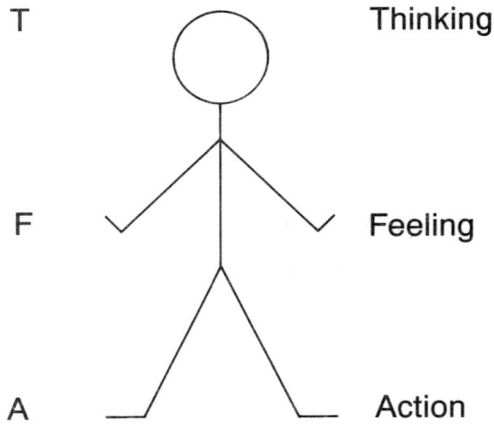

Figure 5.1   TFA Model

vintage sports touring car that is for sale at their local garage.
The first person may perceive and make judgements about the
car from a feelings perspective. They see the shining bodywork,
the sleek lines and contours, gleaming silver chrome head-
lights, walnut facia. They envisage drives down green country
lanes on balmy summer evenings with the warm evening air
rushing through their hair. They display passion, joy and
excitement at the prospect of owning the vehicle. The second
person perceives the car from a thinking, intellectual perspective. They see the car's price tag, problems of garaging and
storage, its non-existent security systems, maintenance costs
and the problem of keeping it clean. Their stance is cool, rational and businesslike. To them it is just another commodity that
will need time, attention and resources.

People, as part of their personality, are more likely to use
greater amounts of either emotion or intellect in reaching decisions, but in periods of great change the feelings factor may
override the thinking factor. If a person is suddenly told that
they are redundant after working for an organization for 20
years, their first reaction is likely to be a charge of emotion. The
type and strength of the feeling will vary depending on the

person and their individual circumstances. A range of emotions could be felt:

- *Anger* Directed towards the organization and its managers that it should have put them in such a position.
- *Happiness* They have at last been released from the shackles that have imprisoned them for the past years.
- *Denial* They do not accept that they have been made redundant and carry on as though nothing has happened.
- *Depression* Their spirits sink and they become lifeless, tired and uninterested.

People react in different ways to change and this reaction will depend upon their vulnerability to the change. One person who is made redundant may regard the event as a minor occurrence if they are young, highly qualified and have substantial financial resources on which to draw. Another person who is aged 50, a single parent supporting two children and paying a large mortgage could regard the redundancy as a disaster and be devastated by it. Therefore the young person may feel nonplussed but the older person may feel great fear and uncertainty and become depressed.

A further influence on how you feel about a change will be the psychological base on which you stand. This base is part of a person's genetic inheritance and their early conditioning and learning. To illustrate this point, people can be seen as living life standing on different psychological foundations. These foundations are illustrated in Figures 5.2 to 5.4.

Figure 5.2 shows a person with firm values, a strong sense of what is right and wrong, an ordered, stable, predictable and controlled life – the Rock Walker. They are likely to have established and firm attitudes to matters that impinge upon their lives. At times a person with such a solid foundation may be described as rigid or dogmatic. The great strength of this type of person is the solid secure base from which they operate. The main weakness of such a solid base is that when circumstances change and require the adoption of new values, perspectives or behaviour such people may have great difficulty in modifying

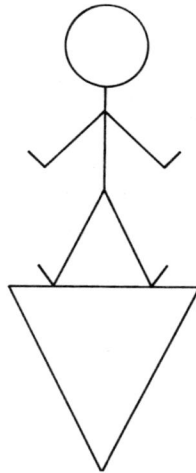

Figure 5.2   The Rock Walker

their base. Therefore if confronted with profound change they may reject it, refuse to cooperate, and become highly resistant and angry.

Figure 5.3   The Swamp Hopper

Figure 5.3 shows a psychological base that is opposite to the Rock Walker. The Swamp Hopper is flexible and fluid and responds to the pressures and demands of the people and

circumstances around them. Unfortunately they can be too flexible and take on too much, sometimes stumbling and falling
into the swamp because they do not have the strong psychological base of the Rock Walker. They may be pushed around by
circumstances and behave like a boat without a rudder. There
may be periods of doubt and uncertainty and in times of rapid
and uncertain change such people suffer from anxiety as the
ground beneath them shifts and they do not have the strength
or structures to hold it together.

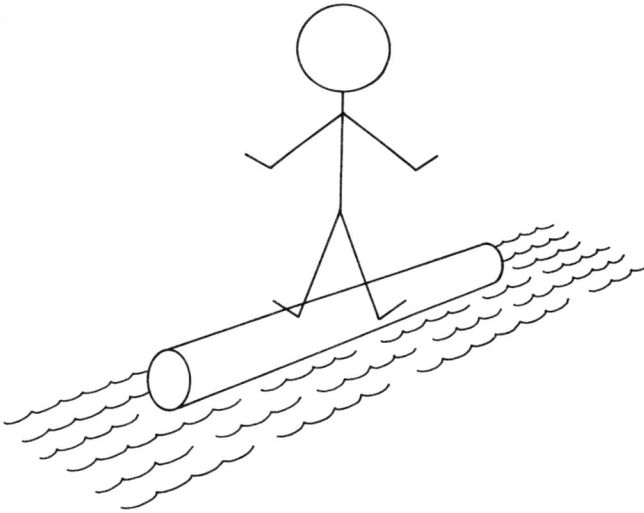

Figure 5.4   The Rapids Rider

The ideal psychological base for a person to develop in order
to manage change successfully is shown in Figure 5.4. The
Rapids Rider can be likened to a lumberjack riding a log down
a river. This base is not as stable and deeply rooted as the Rock
Walker nor as flexible and shaky as the Swamp Hopper. The
Rapids Rider base is stable but at the same time capable of
moving and responding positively to the pressures of life. As
the lumberjack changes position on the log to adapt to the
differing water conditions so the Rapids Riders change their
attitudes, views, perspectives and behaviour to manage the

different circumstances brought about by change.

The Rapids Riders will experience the emotions that can be a consequence of unexpected and rapid change, but unlike the Rock Walker or the Swamp Hopper they will far more easily take control of their feelings and adapt to the change.

Dealing with feelings

To manage change successfully you have to deal with your feelings but this can be difficult because of the nature of emotions. Some feelings are under our control. You may buy yourself a new outfit and feel happy for the next few days. Other feelings are not under our control. You may lose your treasured wristwatch and feel miserable for a week. No matter how much you try to recover from your misery you are unable to.

Other people quickly become aware of your feelings. What a person feels is shown by their behaviour, facial expressions and body language. When you meet a person you quickly judge how they are feeling, whether they are happy, excited, sad, confused, depressed, elated, satisfied and so on.

Feelings can be the route to profound change. A person sees on television the plight of children dying and suffering in Africa. They are left with feelings of despair and compassion which draw them to give up their comfortable and secure job in the West and join an aid agency.

Profound emotions can also override your intellectual and thinking mode in determining behaviour. Think of the spouses and partners who risk their marriages, careers, family and homes by entering into adulterous affairs.

Feelings can be short-term or long-term. A member of the opposite sex may smile at you. This action makes you feel attractive and good about yourself – a short-term feeling with a short-term response. A long-term feeling may be resurrected every time you see a dog. If as a child you were badly bitten by a dog, every time you are close to a dog a feeling of terror and fear may well within you. Your feelings are conditioned by an event that took place 30 years ago.

Feelings are also infectious; they can be quickly transmitted from one person to another. An astute political speaker can make an audience excited and euphoric by using well chosen gestures, rhetoric and vocal technique. In a similar way feelings of pleasure and elation will rapidly spread through the supporters of a football team as their favourite striker scores the winning goal in a match. Opposite feelings can be transmitted if a party is filled with bored introverts, who have little conversation and are waiting for an appropriate time to excuse themselves and go home.

In difficult and confused situations that involve complex human interactions and communication, emotions are often the channel of most truth. In attempting to understand a situation, rather than asking yourself what you `think' you should ask how you `feel'. This question will lead to different insights and perspectives since so much that is hidden by intellectual communication is revealed by feelings.

For many people, an important feature about emotions is that they are difficult to suppress. They usually emerge sooner or later in one form or another. Suppressed feelings can lead to ill health such as ulcers or heart disease. Some people also 'get their own back' on a person who may have wronged them years before.

Exercise 5.1   My feelings

Feelings are a powerful and important factor in the under-standing and management of change. Using the worksheet below, assess yourself against the factors discussed in this section. You will be able to develop a deeper insight into your-self which will help you to manage your change more effectively.

How I live my life

Assess as percentages how you live your life. Allocate 100 percentage points among the three factors, in the proportion that best fits you.

☐ Thinking   Through your head, carefully thinking through your actions and the consequences before taking decisions.

☐ Feeling   Through your heart, following your feelings and making decisions about life on this basis.

☐ Action   Through your actions, like an athlete always active and doing things.

What conclusions do you draw from this analysis? Write them below.

My conclusions

My foundation

Assess the type of foundation on which you stand by ticking the appropriate box.

☐ Rock Walker

☐ Swamp Hopper

☐ Rapids Rider

Write below the conclusions that you draw from your foundation and the implications for the change that you are facing.

My conclusions

My change

My feelings
Analyse your feelings about the change you are now undergoing. Write these below.

My strategy
After considering your feelings, describe the actions that you will take to better handle the change affecting you.

Spot check

Now that you have completed Section 5, identify the three most important points you have learned that will help you to better manage change.

My learning
1
2
3

6 Change and stress

The body never lies.
Martha Graham

When you experience significant change one or several features of your life are altered. You may undergo feelings of instability, uncertainty or loss of control. Often you will suffer personal stress and anxiety. As change is inevitable so stress is inevitable for most people. You have to recognize this fact, recognize the symptoms of stress and take actions to reduce or relieve it.

How stress occurs

Stress always has a cause and typical causes are described in the following case study.

Sally's redundancy
One Friday afternoon in May Sally, an administration manager, is called into her manager's office and told that because of poor trading conditions the company has to cut its costs by reducing the workforce. She is therefore being given a month's notice. The manager is sympathetic and says that the company will help her to find another job and she is free to attend interviews

for jobs and to contact agencies, consultancies and other organizations. The manager praises Sally for her dedication to the company and for the hard work and loyalty she has shown in her five years' service.

Sally is devastated by the news and for the first few hours suffers from intense emotions and physical symptoms She is in a state of shock, feeling dizzy and sick. She has great difficulty in thinking about her situation as her feelings fluctuate between anger, despair, helplessness, fear and resentment. Her colleagues offer their sympathies and tell her that she will soon find another job, but their words have little impact compared with the intensity of her feelings and her uncertainty about the future.

Sally leaves work, drives home in a daze and pours out her feelings to Justin, her partner and father of her two children. Justin, like Sally, was made redundant from his job as a graphic artist and he now works part-time on a freelance basis while looking after the house and caring for the children. Over the weekend Justin and Sally talk about her redundancy; he is a good listener and of great help. Gradually some of her feelings subside as Justin encourages her to think of the main reasons why her redundancy is causing her physical and emotional stress.

She writes them down.

Security
Sally's job has been the main source of income for her, Justin and their two children. Although Justin works as a freelance graphic artist the work is irregular. Without Sally's monthly income the mortgage on the house could not be paid nor the family supported. She and Justin have only a small amount of savings.

Relationships
Sally will miss the very close and friendly relationships that she had built up with her colleagues in the office.

Self-esteem
Sally was hurt that she was the only person in the office to be

made redundant. Why had she been selected? What had she done wrong? She thought that she had been performing well but now her self-esteem and confidence have been gravely damaged.

Status

Sally is worried that being unemployed will affect her status and standing with her friends and in the community. She is a school governor and secretary of the local tennis club.

Sally also feels that her life and general direction have been taken out of her control. Without a secure job and the income that it brings there is an unknown future.

From the moment her manager called her into the office and announced the redundancy Sally has suffered emotional stress and even with Justin's reassuring words she has little sleep over the weekend and wakes in the mornings feeling exhausted.

Over the weekend Sally and Justin develop plans to find Sally another job and if this fails, to secure more freelance work for Justin.

Sally goes to work on the Monday to begin to serve her one month's notice. Although she is slightly reassured after the weekend discussions with Justin, she feels tense and anxious and has started smoking again, a habit that she had stopped six months previously.

The next four weeks are spent diligently applying for jobs and enrolling with job agencies. However, because of the economic climate and the consequent low level of manager vacancy, Sally frequently does not receive an acknowledgement of her application.

She leaves her job after her month's notice and because of the lack of social contact with her work colleagues and the uphill struggle to secure a job she begins to feel depressed. Justin senses the change in Sally and suggests that she should adopt a plan to care for her physical and emotional well-being. This plan involves joining a job search club, taking regular exercise and sticking to a sensible diet and sleeping regime. After two months Sally is still unemployed and she still feels uneasy and apprehensive much of the time. However, her stress and anxiety are under control thanks to the plan that she has adopted. The couple have also been given financial breathing space after discussions with their bank and building society.

Within four months of Sally being made redundant she secures another job which pays more than her previous one. Justin is receiving twice as much freelance work and they have overcome a traumatic stage in their lives and are entering a new phase of family development.

Phases of stress management

As the case study of Sally's redundancy shows, stress management has a number of phases and has to be implemented over a period of time which can range from weeks, months or even years. These phases are general and not all people will react in the same way. Your reactions will depend upon the way in which you view the change, the other changes that are occurring in your life and your physical and mental health.

Much stress occurs when you are uncertain about the future, when you have lost control of your circumstances and do not know what is happening to you. Profound and stressful change has a number of stages and the more you understand them and the way in which you can deal with them the better you will cope with change and the stress associated with it. These stages are detailed below along with an analysis of typical thinking, feeling and acting reactions.

Phase 1   Initial impact
Everybody reacts to profound change and the kind of reaction will depend upon the type of change proposed and the timescale over which it is communicated. When change is seen as damaging to you and is rapidly communicated then your reaction may be a state of immobilization. This reaction occurs when the impact is so great that you suffer physical and emotional trauma. Typical thoughts, feelings and actions are shown in Table 6.1.

Table 6.1

Thoughts	Feelings	Actions
Why has it happened to me?	Anger	Withdraw
Everthing I worked for has	Fear	Cry
disappeared.	Apprehension	Kick things
No holiday this year.	Uncertainty	Provoke arguments
I cannot cope.	Depression	Get drunk
Life is hateful.	Anxiety	Vomit
	Rejection	Talk relentlessly
		Work frantically
		Walk around in a daze

In a state of immobilization you have had your foundations shaken and you may be incapable of carrying on with your normal life.

Phase 2   Denial or minimization

As a means of relieving the stress, pain and threats that the change has incurred, you may attempt to carry on as though nothing has happened. A person who has lost their job may still catch the 7.30 am train to Paddington Station and spend the day reading in the library. A person may minimize the impact of their house burning down by telling themselves that they disliked the house and needed to move anyway. Typical thoughts, feelings and actions of denial or minimization are shown in Table 6.2.

Table 6.2

Thoughts	Feelings	Actions
It will go away if I don't think	Relief	Carry on with the usual
about it.	Anxiety	routine
So my wife left me; she never	Sorrow	Try to be perfect
loved me anyway.	Complacency	Finish uncompleted tasks
Redundancy will give me the	Guilt	Defer to people in authority
opportunity to start again.	Contentment	Comply with people's wishes
I would not have been happy	Peace	Be busy all the time
if I had been promoted to	Suppression	Have a 'clear out'
manager.		

Phase 3   Feelings overflow

Phase 2 is only a temporary relief from the reality of the change that has occurred. The consequences of the change are being avoided and the suppressed feelings have to come out in one form or another. One person may react to this phase in a passive quiet way while another is noisy and aggressive (see Table 6.3).

Table 6.3

Thoughts	Feelings	Actions
It is real.	Anger	Withdraw from people and
It won't go away.	Depression	social situations
My life with have to change.	Loneliness	Irritability
I am worthless.	Sadness	Short-temperedness
I am in trouble.	Worthlessness	Aggression
	Vulnerability	Distant with people

Phase 4   Letting go

A person at Phase 4 is resigning themselves to the fact that the change has happened and that there is little they can do about it. Phase 3 has enabled them to purge their systems of their feelings, which has had a calming and therapeutic effect. You begin to realize that your best strategy is to discard the unwanted and painful aspects of your old behaviour and routines and discover new ones. The thinking, feeling and actions associated with this phase are shown in Table 6.4.

Table 6.4

Thinking	Feelings	Actions
Forget about the past.	Apprehension	Begin looking for opportunities
I have to build something	Uncertainty	Make new friends and
new.	Excitement	acquaintances
I must decide on the best	Sorrow	Sever ties with the old
direction to follow.	Reflection	Take more care of self
Things must change.	Guilt	Buy new clothes
Life will never be the same	Fear	
again.		

Phase 5 Experimenting and testing

At this phase you will have thought of one or various options that can follow to make up for the loss you have suffered in the change and you will be in the process of testing them out. The testing will be specific to the loss encountered. A person who was forced to take a demotion will be testing the new job. Someone who accepted redundancy may be exploring another career, considering studying for a higher level qualification or exploring the route to self-employment. A person who has separated from their partner may be testing a different lifestyle and new relationships. The thinking, feelings and actions of this phase are shown in Table 6.5.

Table 6.5

Thinking	*Feelings*	*Actions*
A new era of my life is about to begin.	Hopefulness	Trying new things
	Excitement	Getting out and about
I will try various options and see which one succeeds.	Going forward	Meeting new people
	Enjoyment	Adapting to new surroundings
Life could be different and exciting.	Dissatisfaction	Developing relationships
	Apprehension	Exploring new activities
It isn't too bad.	Satisfaction	Withdrawing from
Why didn't I do this before?	Vulnerability	unsatisfactory situations
This isn't for me.		

Phase 6 Building the future

From Phase 5 a future pathway will be selected and established. The old should be abandoned, although parts of it will still remain. If you have carefully chosen your new future you will be engrossed in developing it and making it work. Many of the intense feelings of the first phases will have subsided as you begin the new era (Table 6.6).

Table 6.6

Thinking	Feelings	Actions
Life is good.	Excitement	Working hard at the new
Why was I so depressed when	Pleasure	Looking for further
change occurred?	Worry	opportunities
When change comes again I	Joy	Learning new skills
will know how to cope.	Contentment	Developing new networks
There is no point in having	Apprehension	of friends
regrets.	Satisfaction	Cementing relationships
I miss some aspects of the past.	Reassurance	Building up resources

Stress

Stress occurs in human beings when we feel under threat and unable to cope. At a primitive level human beings facing danger undergo a change in their physiological and psychological mechanisms. These changes include increased heart rate, a release of adrenaline into the bloodstream, sweating, faster breathing and an increase in alertness and perceptions. These changes were ideal in primitive times when people were in danger for minutes or hours, when they had to 'fight' or 'take flight', but they are inappropriate for people who feel under longer term threat. A constant state of alertness is unhealthy for the average human being and can lead to psychological and physical breakdown.

The symptoms of stress can be broken down into two main categories: physical and mental. Some examples of symptoms are provided in Table 6.7.

You and stress

Stress and its effects on you is personal and individual. A situation that is highly stressful to one person can be exhilarating to another because of differences in personality and psychological make-up. Futhermore there are often different circumstances involved. For example, one person who is made

Table 6.7   Symptoms of stress

Physical	*Mental*
Sweating	Apprehension
Palpitations	Depression
Dry throat	Aggression
High blood pressure	Worry
Indigestion	Uncertainty
Headaches	Tiredness
Taut muscles	Apathy
Frequent bowel and bladder movements	Memory loss
Lowered sex drive	Lack of concentration
Blurred vision	Irritability
Dizziness	Inability to cope
Crying	Tension
Disturbed sleep patterns	Dreaming
Fainting	Feeling a failure

redundant may welcome the freedom that it brings to start another career. Another person may be devastated as it just adds to their current misfortune, such as financial problems and family bereavement.

Some amount of stress is necessary to arouse a person to the level where they can deal with the change facing them. The stress is in fact beneficial. A manager who is making a presentation to a gathering of 200 important customers should be aroused sufficiently to be enthusiastic, perceptive and alert. If she were not aroused and presented in a boring and uninteresting way, her speech interrupted by yawns, then she would be doing a disservice to herself, her organization and her customers. If she were over-aroused and suffering from a headache, loss of concentration, dizziness and stuttering, thereby giving a disjointed presentation, then she could have a negative effect on her audience. However, in these circumstances she may gain sympathy from some of the listeners.

A high state of arousal becomes too stressful when it is prolonged and affects your feeling of well-being and eventually your health.

When you are affected by change you should ask yourself three important questions:

- Am I experiencing stress?
- Is the stress adversely affecting me?
- What can I do about it?

Dealing with stress

To relieve stress you have to look to both short-term and long-term solutions. Referring to Sally's redundancy, the long-term solution to her problem was to find another job so that she could support the family and regain status and esteem in the community. However, she had to take measures to alleviate the stress in the four months that it took to find a new job. The steps that she took which also contributed to the long-term solutions were:

- She expresses her feelings to her partner Justin.
- Justin acted as a counsellor.
- The discussions with Justin identified the reasons why Sally felt so bad about the redundancy.
- With Justin, Sally developed a plan to find a job.
- Sally began activities to take care of her mental and physical well-being: regular exercise, sensible diet, strict sleeping routine and the job search club.
- Discussions with the bank and building society about finances.
- Justin tried to secure more work.

After four months Sally overcame her problem and started to live life again as normal.

There are many techniques for reducing or alleviating stress and some of these are described below.

Emotional

- Share your problems and stresses with a close friend or relative.
- Join a stress therapy counselling group.

- Study video and audio tapes on stress management.
- Read books on stress and stress management.
- Practise meditation or yoga.
- Escape your stress, go on a holiday.
- Join new clubs and societies.
- Widen your circle of friends.
- Develop new interests.
- Make contact with some of your old friends.
- Listen to relaxing music.
- Drink alcohol in moderation.
- Take up cooking and invite friends around for meals.
- Buy yourself something attractive.

Health

- Carefully monitor your drinking and smoking habits.
- Go for regular walks.
- Start swimming.
- Join a health club.
- Monitor your diet and eat regularly.
- Ensure you get sufficient sleep.
- 'Cat nap' for 15 minutes when you feel stressed or tired.
- Visit your doctor for advice or medication.
- Join a golf, tennis, squash, badminton club, etc.
- Say no to extra work and pressure.
- Use all your leave.
- Buy an answer phone for weekends and evenings.
- Use the car less and start cycling.

Problem related

- Plan a longer term strategy for solving your problem.
- Talk to people who have had a similar problem.
- Seek professional advice.
- Discuss financial issues with experts such as accountants, bank managers and mortgage advisors.
- Read books to gain insights and advice.
- Join a self-help group.

- Contact the citizens advice bureau.
- Visit the local library for information.
- Work closely with a friend or colleague on your problem.
- Consider the consequences of doing nothing. Would the problem go away?

Managing your stress

Now that you have read this section on stress you should identify your own stress symptoms and plan to reduce or alleviate them. Describe your symptoms below.

My stress symptoms	
Physical	Mental

Having identified your symptoms, assess the impact the stress is having on you and the normal functioning of your life. Do this by ticking the box that is appropriate to you on the scale below.

I understand the stress affecting me. It is under control and I am finding more effective ways of managing it even better.

1	2	3	4	5	6	7

The stress has completely taken over my life. It is with me all the time and I some-times think I will not be able to cope.

Now plan to reduce your stress by drawing up a schedule for the next six months. Involve one or several other people in the plan as they will give advice, support and encouragement. This support will be particularly important at times when your spirits and motivation are low. Refer to page 64 and consider using some of the methods and techniques for dealing with stress discussed there. Set out your plan on the exercise sheet on the following page.

My plan	People helping me
What I will start doing immediately.	
What I will do over the next six months.	
How will I be. Describe how you will think, feel and act when you have reduced your level of stress.	

Spot check

Now that you have completed Section 6, identify the three most important points you have learned about dealing with stress.

My learning
1
2
3

7 Attitudes to change

If you look at life one way, there is always cause for alarm.
Elizabeth Bowen

Sections 1 and 2 showed that you must learn to live with constant change as change is inevitable. You have to decide whether you embrace change and find it exciting and full of opportunities or whether you resist change and see it as threatening and something to be avoided. Embracing and adapting to change is the progressive healthy position to take. Resisting change leads to internal turmoil and stress and in the longer term is counter-productive to you and the organization in which you work.

The development of attitudes

Individuals have differing capabilities to absorb new ideas and learn new skills and behaviours. One of the main reasons for this is that we are all surrounded by a hypothetical change shield as shown in Figure 7.1.

This change shield is the mechanism that each of us erects around us for protection from the outside world. Within the shield we feel fairly secure having built a psychological envi-

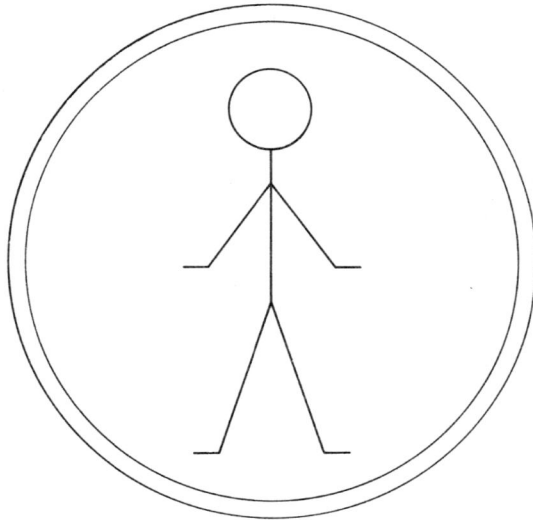

Figure 7.1   Change shield

ronment that we are able to manage. When operating within the shield we are able to cope, as we are dealing with situations that have been tested and rehearsed. If forced to operate outside this shield in new, unfamiliar or difficult circumstances, apprehension, uncertainty and stress levels are increased.

A method of maintaining the change shield is through defence mechanisms. A defence mechanism is a device that you use to eliminate or reduce what one perceives as potentially damaging influences. There are many defence mechanisms – some of the most common are:

- *Projection* Ascribing to others your own unadmitted desires and impulses. The quarrelsome person who accuses others of being aggressive.
- *Denial* Refusing to accept that an event has occurred – 'My husband is not having an affair with a female colleague.'
- *Reaction formation* Expressing the opposite situation to that which is present – 'Sara is not a calculating untrustworthy person, she is warm, open and honest.'
- *Intellectualizing* Withholding the hurtful and damaging

emotional details of an event by viewing it in a calm rational manner – 'My daughter has crashed my new car. She has learned a great deal from the accident and will be a far better driver in future.'

- *Withdrawal*   Refusing to be involved in an emotional or distressing situation – 'You can dismiss Brian if you wish but don't involve me. I want nothing to do with it.'
- *Displacement*   Discharging strong feelings such as anger or aggression on to some other unrelated object or person, such as breaking a mirror or shouting at your children.
- *Diversion*   Reducing attention to a situation by diverting yourself and others away from it by telling jokes or creating laughter.

There are many forms of defence mechanisms and almost all forms of human behaviour can be used in this way.

The change shield also features some other important characteristics, for example to some people it is invisible and they are not aware of its existence. The defence mechanisms operate at a subconscious level and we are unaware when and how frequently we use them.

Other people may not be aware of the nature of our defence shields. It depends upon how open we are with them and how far we allow them to see our fears and weaknesses and the way in which we protect ourselves. Often we are selective with what we reveal and what we hide, depending on the people and circumstances involved. We may reveal to one person that we are afraid and have a horror of giving a talk to a small group of people and yet we do not reveal this information to another person whom we trust less.

People develop shields of different thickness. One person may have a thick shield and be very closed. They reveal little about themselves and others never get on close terms with them. Another person's shield may be thin. They are open, responsive and sharing and people get to know them very quickly.

One of the main determinants of the type of shield that a person erects around themselves is the degree of personal security and vulnerability that they feel. If they constantly feel threatened by their environment then they will erect a thick, strong shield that is capable of repelling powerful attacks. On the other hand, if people feel able to deal effectively with their environment and respond positively and successfully their shield will be less robust and more adaptable.

The shield develops in a person's formative years and it changes in response to life's experiences. If a person has been involved in a painful personal relationship which has left them bruised and hurt they may build a thick impenetrable shield which will not allow in any new relationships for fear of further hurt. Another person who has had several warm and nourishing personal relationships may be far more open to establishing new associations with people.

The significance of the change shield to a person's attitude is that the more robust and impenetrable it is the more likely that a person's attitude to change will be rigid or negative.

Attitudes and behaviour

Attitudes are very important to understanding and managing change since your attitude will determine the way in which you perceive the change and the way that you react and behave. This is illustrated by the APB cycle in Figure 7.2.

The Attitude, Perception and Behaviour (APB) cycle shows that your attitude to change is influenced by two important factors, your personality and the nature of the change affecting you. As already discussed, different types of people will construct around them different kinds of change shield. These shields will predispose a person to think about change in a certain way. The other factor is how the nature of the change reacts with the personality to set the attitude. Thus if a change was proposed to cut the number of staff running an office by 50 per cent with little offered as compensation then most people in the office would develop a negative attitude to the change irrespective of the type of change shield that they wore. The attitude may, however, be the reverse if most people in the

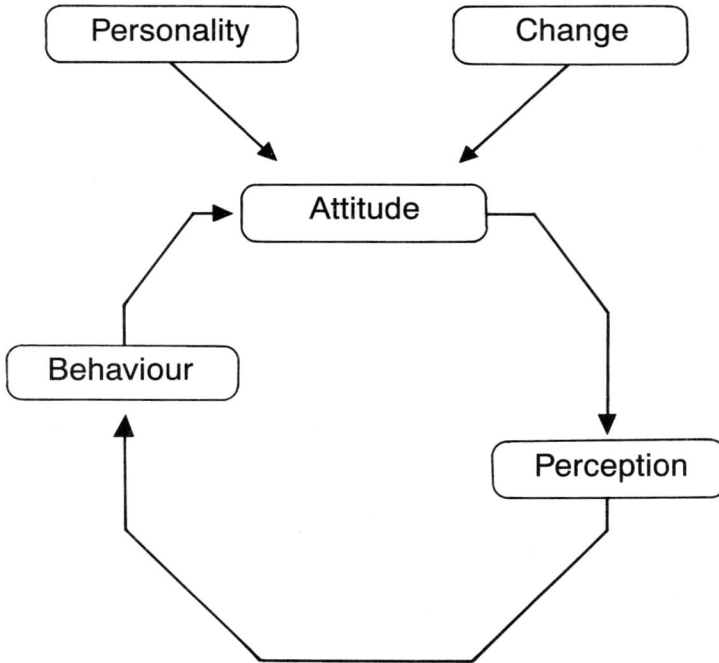

Figure 7.2 The APB cycle

office were underutilized, bored and continually waiting for work.

In the same office if the change proposed was a new computerized system for processing orders then opposing attitudes to the change could develop. Those people with flexible change shields and knowledge of computers might adopt a positive and receptive attitude while those people with little computer knowledge and rigid change shields might develop a negative attitude to the change.

Your attitude to change is vital because, as shown in the APB cycle, it influences your perception. A negative attitude will lead to selectively choosing negative, disruptive or controversial aspects of the change rather than positive features and benefits. This effect can be shown in the example above of the introduction of the new computerized system for processing orders. The person with the positive attitude will perceive that the change will result in a more effective service, fewer human errors, quicker data retrieval, comprehensive recording of complaints, easier completion of reports and so on. The person with the negative attitude will see the exorbitant cost of the system, computers taking people's jobs, the problems of computer failure, eye strain and fatigue encountered from working with screens and the enormous amount of new knowledge and skills to be learned by everyone. The attitude therefore acts as a filter on information, building up a database and a case either for or against the change.

After perception the APB cycle focuses on behaviour. What you perceive will determine how you behave. Thus the person with the positive attitude to the computer system perceives all of its positive features and advantages and consequently behaves accordingly. They will be eager and enthusiastic to learn the system and invest their time and energy ensuring that it operates effectively. They will help others to understand and learn the system and enjoy the challenge of sorting out the problems that occur. The person with the negative attitude, if they have chosen not to leave or transfer to another department, will be a reluctant learner. They may lack the desire and motivation to experiment with the system and understand its full potential. The system is learned and operated under duress. It is a job that has to be done. Eventually, as the negative person learns the system they may come to appreciate the benefits it brings to them and their customers, and attitude change could take place. They progress round the cycle, altering their perceptions and then their behaviour. The following exercises will help you to assess and understand your attitude to the change that occurs in your job or workplace.

Exercise 7.1 My attitude to change

Below are a number of statements. The statements are in pairs separated by a 7-point scale. Read each pair of statements and decide the degree to which you agree with them. For example considering the first statements:

1 Most change is unnecessary. We change for change's sake.

1	2	3	4	5	6	7

Most change is necessary. We have to keep ahead.

If you think that 'Most change is unnecessary' then tick box 1. On the other hand, if you think that 'Most change is necessary' then tick box 7. If your view lies somewhere between the two statements then tick the appropriate box.

Now complete the exercise.

1 Most change is unnecessary. We change for change's sake.

1	2	3	4	5	6	7

Most change is necessary. We have to stay ahead.

2 Most people are worse off from change.

1	2	3	4	5	6	7

Most people benefit from change.

3 Change is a disruptive and stressful process which should be avoided if possible.

1	2	3	4	5	6	7

Change is a beneficial and exciting process which has to be integrated into your job.

4   Change takes the satisfaction and enjoyment out of your job.

1	2	3	4	5	6	7

Change builds interest, motivation and enjoyment into your job.

5   Faced with new situations I often feel unsure and insecure.

1	2	3	4	5	6	7

Faced with new situations I always feel confident and secure.

6   In the past I have found change to be disruptive and detrimental to me.

1	2	3	4	5	6	7

In the past I have found change to be advantageous and rewarding to me.

7   Constant change demoralizes people.

1	2	3	4	5	6	7

Constant change motivates people.

8   People would describe me as a 'closed' person.

1	2	3	4	5	6	7

People would describe me as an 'open' person.

9   Most people just want to come to work and get on with their jobs rather than changing all the time.

1	2	3	4	5	6	7

Most people are happy with job changes as they are necessary to secure the future.

10   Senior managers make all the decisions about change and employees have little say.

1	2	3	4	5	6	7

All employers are involved in decision-making at the appropriate time.

11 I like working in
a stable, predictable
and routine
environment.

1	2	3	4	5	6	7

I like working in a
fast-moving, ever-
changing
environment.

12 Other organizations
manage change
much better than us.

1	2	3	4	5	6	7

Our organization
manages change
systematically and
effectively.

13 I am a person who
makes decisions
based on my
strong beliefs and
principles.

1	2	3	4	5	6	7

I am a person who
makes decisions
based on the
circumstances of each
case.

14 Senior managers are
the only winners
from change
programmes.

1	2	3	4	5	6	7

Everybody is a winner
from change
programmes.

15 The result of change
is that you work
harder for less
reward.

1	2	3	4	5	6	7

The results of change
are that work is more
satisfying and
rewarding.

Scoring the exercise

Add your scores on each of the 15 factors. Write the total score
in the box below and then compare your total score with the
ranges shown.

Total score:

Score	Interpretation
105–75	**High** You have a very positive attitude to change. You understand that change is now a way of life that must be accepted and managed. You do not find change threatening and see many of the benefits that change can bring.
74–45	**Medium** This is an average score and indicates that while not directly opposing change you have reservations about its benefits to you and your organization. You should examine your attitude to aspects of change to which you are opposed and try to make improvements.
44–15	**Low** You find change stressful and disruptive. You are opposed to change and the effect that it has on you and your job. You believe that much change is unnecessary and badly managed. This negative attitude prevents you progressing and successfully meeting the challenges of the future.

Developing a PCA (Positive Change Attitude)

For organizations to survive and for people to have secure and satisfying jobs a positive and enthusiastic attitude to change is necessary. The most salutary lesson to be learned about change is that organizations that do not change in the long term do not survive. If you want to increase your PCA there are a number of steps that you should follow.

Step 1	Consider the industries and organizations that have not survived or have been drastically reduced in size because they did not successfully embrace and manage change. Write three examples below.
Step 2	Describe the state of your organization in five years' time if you did not change. Write your description below.
Step 3	Briefly describe the kind of change shield that surrounds you as described on page 71. Consider how your friends and colleagues would describe you.
Step 4	Identify the three most important factors that prevent you from developing a more PCA.

Step 5   What will happen to you if you do not adopt a more PCA?
Write a description below.

Step 6   Set out an action plan to develop a PCA.

My action plan

Spot check

Now that you have completed Section 7 identify and describe the three most important points you have learned about attitudes to change.

My learning
1
2
3

8   Anchors

Unless you find some sort of loyalty you cannot find unity and peace in your active living.
Josiah Royce

When you experience significant change some or perhaps much of your life will be transformed by it. Some change may undermine the foundations of your life and when this happens you can be confused and in a state of limbo, an unhealthy and stressful state to be. In this condition points of stability, or anchors, must be identified and developed. These anchors will form part of the stable base from which to manage the change and progress.

Different forms of change

Different forms of change require different kinds of anchor. An anchor may satisfy a need at the time and then be abandoned or pulled up once it has served its purpose. The following case studies explore several different kinds of change and the types of anchor that were chosen.

Continuous overlapping change

Ralph is a middle manager in a large food processing plant. Over the past five years he has been subjected to wave upon wave of change which has left him disrupted, confused and in a state of uncertainty. The waves of change that Ralph has had to adopt to are:

- Acquisition of the company by a large international group. There were rumours that the plant would be closed and production transferred to Holland. In the meantime 250 employees were made redundant and several of the product lines were dismantled. Ralph was given responsibility for two production units when his colleague was made redundant.
- A cost-cutting exercise was introduced into the plant with the aim of increasing efficiency. External consultants were recruited and Ralph was appointed as a member of a steering committee to debate and agree suitable cuts.
- A new plant manager was appointed who quickly re-organized the management structure and declared 30 middle managers redundant. Ralph was transferred to the production planning department. He spent the next three months learning advanced computer skills and production planning techniques.
- Senior management decided to implement a teamworking philosophy in the plant. Production units were organized around self-managing teams. Ralph was appointed as a part-time team facilitator to help develop teamworking.
- Business started to boom and orders increased. Two new production lines were added and everybody was extremely busy. Ralph was seconded to develop and introduce a new planning system and train people in its use.
- The parent company decided to acquire an international quality standard award. All managers had to develop procedures and manuals. Ralph was given responsibility for all planning matters.

During the past five years Ralph has been subjected to one change initiative after another. Apart from doing his everyday job he had to apply energy, resources and time to at least two and sometimes three other areas of priority. To achieve these aims Ralph works very long hours and takes work home every evening. He frequently calls into the plant on a weekend. With this amount of change, pressure and stress Ralph could easily break down and the job become too much for him to handle. However, Ralph has some strong anchor points in his life which enable him to keep a sense of perspective and balance:

- Josie, a caring and understanding wife, who fully appreciates the pressure and stress of Ralph's job and tries to ensure that her actions do not add to them. Ralph recognizes the important role played by Josie and is extremely grateful for her support. He frequently expresses this with many small treats and his love and affection.
- After working in such a highly pressurized and changing environment, Ralph has to escape and allow his mind to settle. Every Sunday morning he is up early fishing at the local carp lake. Four hours sitting alone watching his float and observing the wild life are extremely therapeutic. This experience enables him to put things into perspective. Work is only one aspect of his life and it should not be allowed to consume him.
- Every Friday evening Ralph meets his brothers Jason and David for a game of snooker and a drink. The three of them share a similar kind of humour and the affection of brothers. They talk about their families, work, common interests, holidays, friends and so on. If Ralph is concerned about anything he can discuss it with his brothers. They are a valuable source of advice and help him a great deal.

Radical shock change

Six months ago Annie's world was shattered. Her husband of seven years, Simon, informed her that he wanted the marriage to end, he no longer loved her and he was going to live with his new love Suzy. Simon left leaving Annie heartbroken and in shock. The main reason for Annie's hurt and despair was that Simon's infidelity had come as a complete surprise to her. Their relationship had appeared to be fairly stable and their life together was relatively harmonious apart from occasional quarrels. Occasionally Simon was distant and off-hand, but Annie had attributed this mood change to the pressure and stress of his work. Simon was a photocopy machine salesman. He covered a territory in the East Midlands of England. He frequently made early starts to visit clients at 9 am and was often out until 7 pm or 8 pm in the evenings. There was always pressure to achieve sales targets.

Annie worked as a cashier in a building society. She had a regular 9 am to 5 pm job in the town centre which enabled her to have the time and routine to organize the household. Since their marriage they had purchased a house with a mortgage; it was now furnished and Annie was looking forward to starting a family.

Before Simon left he explained that his new love Suzy was a member of the salesforce and that their relationship had developed and grown as they worked together. It was six months since Simon had left and Annie was now beginning to accept her changed situation and was learning to cope with the pain that Simon had caused. Various anchors in her life had assisted this process:

- As soon as Simon left Annie contacted her best friend, Louise, who came to stay with her for several days. As Annie cried and talked and sobbed and shouted, Louise listened with sympathy and understanding. Louise realized that Annie was in a state of shock and that she would have to cope with the shock and stabilize her emotions before she would be able to think rationally about her position. Louise also advised Annie to seek the advice of a doctor for medication to calm her down and help her sleep at night. After Annie overcame the initial shock of the break from Simon, Louise was always at hand to give advice, help and counselling.
- Annie soon realized that as a single person her job would assume a greater significance in her life. With Simon gone she now had to support herself and perhaps her job would be her only source of income in the future. She therefore planned in the next year to enrol for education courses

that would qualify her for more senior positions in the organization.

- As the months passed Annie's feelings for Simon slowly changed to distaste and at times even hatred. She felt that she had done nothing wrong and it was Simon who had broken the relationship and in an abrupt manner. This behaviour had been unforgivable. This change of feeling and attitude towards Simon gave her a foundation to break with the tender and loving feelings of the past.
- Annie joined the local amateur dramatic society with her colleague Amanda from the building society. This meant she went out two evenings a week to rehearsals followed by a drink in the local pub. There were also productions of the plays at weekends. This activity gave Annie a new interest and a different circle of friends.

Insidious creeping change

Joe is the training manager of a new and fast-growing business that runs pubs and restaurants. He is tired and feels worn out. He has little energy or enthusiasm, has difficulty sleeping at night, and even greater difficulty getting up in the morning. He is drinking too much and is irritable with his wife and children. In the past months Joe has suffered from influenza and several heavy colds. During these illnesses he has felt particularly low and depressed but he has managed to continue working. Because of work pressures Joe has so far not taken any holiday this year although his wife and children went on holiday with his wife's sister.

It has been a particularly gruelling week for Joe and although the alarm has rung at the usual time of 6.30 am, on this Thursday morning he feels too ill and tired to get up and go to work. He asks his wife to contact his boss and to arrange an appointment with his doctor.

The diagnosis of the doctor is exactly as Joe had suspected, stress and gross overwork had gradually, physically and mentally worn him down. He was given some medication and advised to take a complete break from his work and routines for two weeks. Joe took this advice and quickly arranged a holiday for himself and his wife. Before going on holiday he decided to trace back the circumstances that had led to this predicament. He reflected upon his life in the past years.

When Joe was appointed training manager two years previously the company was embarking on an ambitious expansion plan of opening 25 new units a year. This development was led by a new and dynamic managing director who enthused everyone with her drive, dedication and business acumen. It was Joe's job to ensure that the managers and staff who would run the pubs and restaurants were trained to carry out their roles effectively. Joe ran courses for all staff in the Head Office and also in the units, often at weekends or in the evenings. Timings and deadlines were precise as it was unthinkable for a new unit to begin operating with inefficient staff. There was also considerable travelling involved in Joe's work as some of the units were over 100 miles from his home.

For the first year Joe was totally absorbed running courses, training staff and acting as a coach and mentor to the new employees. His home telephone number and his mobile phone number were circulated to all employees and trainers. This easy access meant that Joe would be contacted to answer queries and solve problems late at night and over the weekend. Joe was on call 18 hours a day seven days a week.

In Joe's second year his workload increased as new systems were introduced, managers and staff left existing units and had to be replaced and trained, and the opening of the units continued. Life became more hectic and pressurized and Joe began to feel the strain. However, he continued throughout the year by working longer hours and managed to carry out the planned programme. In the last six months of the year Joe noticed a marked deterioration in his output and standards, with memory lapses and the inability to respond to people's requests for help. His performance became even worse until the fateful Thursday morning when he could take no more.

After this analysis Joe, through discussion with his wife, decided the way in which he would organize his life and the anchors and stability points he would introduce to prevent another breakdown. They agreed on the following actions:

- Joe would discuss with his boss the appointment of an assistant training manager who could share the workload. They would also arrange between them an 'on call' rota and publicize it to the organization so that they would have some evenings and weekends free from telephone calls.
- Rather than Joe travelling home after every late night training session he would sometimes stay overnight in a hotel. This would relieve the stress of travelling and allow a good night's sleep.
- A family holiday would be arranged at the beginning of every year and under no circumstances would it be changed or cancelled.
- Joe would start to play golf with his friend Colin as a means of creating another interest and getting some exercise.
- A family trip would be arranged once a month to a leisure centre, theme park, the theatre, the cinema, a rural walk and so on. A monthly outing would be good for the family and help Joe to relax.

Different kinds of anchor

Different people will require different kinds of anchor depending upon the form of change that is affecting them and the way in which they are coping. There are various types of anchor.

Friendship
A friendship anchor is another person or persons to be a companion for discussions or social activities. The main purpose of the anchor is to provide another interest or diversion to keep the change in the correct perspective, with appropriate discussions and helpful advice being given. The social activities may be many and varied depending upon the interests of the people concerned.

Spiritual
A person seeking a spiritual anchor may have been so transformed by the change that they require a new foundation on

which to rebuild their lives. They may develop a new religious faith or join a church. Other spiritual anchors can be found in movements or sects. These anchors enable a person to believe in something that is far greater than everyday material living and which gives meaning to life.

Relationships

A relationship anchor is where a person builds up a new relationship to replace one that has been destroyed or seriously damaged. The relationship acts as foundation for new activities or directions. A typical relationship anchor would be the taking of a new partner to help overcome a divorce.

Fitness

A person suffering the stress and emotional upheaval of change may pursue the fitness route to help them manage the change. At some stage they will realize that the stress and its associated physical and psychological consequences are having an adverse effect on their health. They therefore begin a strict regime of exercise, jogging, gym visits, swimming and so on. This gives them greater resilience to cope with the change and also provides a different focus in their lives.

Interest

An interest anchor is the building up of an existing interest or establishing a new interest. As with some of the other anchors this interest provides a new and different focus in life which helps to reduce the uncertainty or stress of the change. An interest anchor can be almost anything in which human beings become involved, for example watercolour painting, playing golf, fishing, gardening, football, aerobics, learning a foreign language and so on.

Self-development

Radical change often provides the impetus for a person to evaluate themselves and take stock of what they have so far achieved in their lives. This assessment may lead to a complete change of direction. The certificate in French that a person was studying for is transformed into a future French Degree and a job teaching French. A person who spent twenty years in an insurance office before being made redundant decides to make his photography hobby into a business.

Counselling

Some change emotionally damages a person and they would have great difficulty overcoming it without extensive help and counselling. In these circumstances it is essential to have a counselling anchor. This anchor can be provided by friends or professional counselling services available through doctors, psychologists and help groups.

Exercise 8.1　Identifying your anchors

You have read three examples of people experiencing different forms of change and then identifying and developing anchors to help them cope with the change. We have also defined different kinds of anchor. Now identify the anchors in your life and consider how they can assist you to overcome your change. Complete the following stages of the exercise.

Change affecting me
Briefly summarize in a short paragraph the change affecting you.

My change

Established anchors

Reflecting on the anchors used by Annie, Ralph and Joe, write down the anchors that you will use to help you overcome your change. Alongside each anchor define exactly what you will do to make the anchor work effectively for you.

Anchors	Actions to be taken

New anchors

Having considered your established anchors you may have decided that they do not adequately cater for all your needs and therefore new or different forms must be established. Define your new anchors below and describe how you will develop them.

New anchors	Actions to be taken

Spot check

Now that you have completed Section 8, identify and describe the three most important points you have learned about change anchors.

My learning
1
2
3

9 Transition periods

All changes, even the most longed for, have their melancholy for what we leave behind us is a part of ourselves; we must die one life before we can enter into another.
Anatole France

When you undergo profound change you must understand that the change from one set of circumstances to another involves many stages and takes time. Often the feelings, relationships, attitudes and behaviours of the old situation have to be abandoned and new ones learned. There is a transition from the old to the new which may be very emotional, evoking feelings of excitement, pain, depression, anger, happiness, resentment, uncertainty and so on. This transition must be managed.

Transition periods

The change from one set of circumstances to another takes time. The length of time will depend upon many factors, including your personality, the type of change, the personal losses and gains accruing from the change, the support received and your attitude to the change. To begin to explore these transition periods complete Exercise 9.1.

Exercise 9.1   **Transition periods**

A number of occurrences that affect people and cause them to change are listed below.

Occurrence	Estimated time
Redundancy: finding a new job and settling into it	
Winning £3m. in the National Lottery	
Being offered another job at twice your current salary	
Losing your spouse or partner in a tragic road accident	
Resigning from your job to become a student	
Losing a limb in an accident	
Being left £100,000 in a relative's will	
Your spouse or partner leaving you for another person	
Your house burning down while on holiday	
Being told by your boss that your promotion application has been successful	

For each occurrence estimate how long you think it would take you to come to terms with the occurrence and then manage your transition to the new situation. Unless you have actually encountered the specific occurrences you can only guess what your reactions would be and the time involved. However, you know yourself and your reaction to events and the way in which you manage change. Therefore put an estimated time against each occurrence:

Understanding your estimated times

Different people completing Exercise 9.1 will have given very different estimated times. Some people will have been unable to give what they regard as reliable times. Other people may have been unable to give any times at all because they could not envisage the situation or the factors that influence the length of the transition period. Some of these factors are described below.

Effects of the change
One of the characteristics of a change is that although a person is fully aware of their present circumstances because they are living and experiencing them every day, they often have only a vague picture of their future. A person realizes that changes are happening but they are uncertain about how the changes will continue and what their eventual outcome will be. Therefore the person who is made redundant and has to seek another job, in the beginning often has no certain vision of their future. They set a general direction in which to move which may occur. On the other hand the vision and plans may be impossible to achieve and have to be abandoned and another direction planned. Even when a change plan works successfully it will take time for a person to feel in control and relatively stable in their new environment.

Surprise
Another factor that affects the length of the transition period is the element of surprise in the person receiving the information about the change. The greater the surprise the less time a

person will have had to prepare themselves. Therefore a person who is told without any prior warning that the organization for which they work is to close down the next day is likely to be more shocked and have a longer transition period than the person who was given six months' notice of a possible closure. The first person has suddenly lost a vital part of their living experience whereas the second person has lived with the possibility of closure and has been able to prepare a plan for the future.

Readiness

Some people are psychologically more ready for change than other people. A person may have reached a stage in their life where they require and may be actively seeking a change. For example, the person who has had a tempestuous relationship with their partner may feel little regret when they sever the relationship. Similarly the manager who is asked to work in another country may welcome the change if the existing job lacked challenge and they were seeking new opportunities. When the readiness for change is high a person may find the change stimulating and enjoyable. If the readiness for change is low then the change process can be difficult and stressful with a long transition period.

Emotional attachment

The emotional attachment of a person to a changed event will have a considerable impact on the length of the transition period. A parent losing a child in a tragic accident may never recover from the shock. They may be able to carry on with their life but will always bear the scars of the event. The emotional attachment to their offspring is so intense that they never lose it. Low or minimal emotional attachment can greatly reduce the transition period.

Disruption

The amount of physical disruption that a person undergoes will affect the transition period. A person may in a short period of time lose their job, divorce and move home. These changes will cause considerable disruption that lasts for several years. Intense emotional stress will be created which will be increased by the instability of being unemployed and seeking somewhere to live.

Gains

The transition period may be reduced considerably if the change brings with it personal gains to the individual. For example a UK sales manager may be promoted to European Sales Director. Everything about the change may be positive: a greater challenge, living in Paris, higher status, a larger car, a more sophisticated lifestyle and a more interesting network of colleagues. If all goes well the transition period should be very happy and short in duration. The organization would attend to all of the person's physical and material requirements and the move itself should bring great joy and contentment.

Losses

Change often results in a person losing rather than winning. The losses may be material: a comfortable home, possessions, a company car and a steady income. Other losses can be status, self-esteem, position in the community, the respect of friends and professional standing in the eyes of colleagues. In addition there are the emotional losses of broken relationships. Many people faced with change would hope eventually to recover these losses as they adapt to the change and move on. In some situations it may be possible to recover all the losses but many people will have to settle for less. The process of accepting and managing the loss will extend the transition period.

Exercise 9.2   Transition factors

This exercise will help you relate the transition factors to your own change. After completing the exercise you will have a better understanding of your change, which will enable you to manage it more effectively.

Below are the seven factors with a 4-point scale. Tick one box for each factor, the box that most closely represents your view of the change affecting you. If necessary review the definitions of the factors given in the previous section.

Effects of the change	fully known	partly known	mainly unknown	totally unknown
	1	2	3	4
Surprise to you	no surprise	slight surprise	some surprise	complete surprise
	1	2	3	4
Your readiness	fully prepared	partly prepared	mainly un-prepared	totally un-prepared
	1	2	3	4
Emotional attachment	no attachment	slight attachment	some attachment	deep attachment
	1	2	3	4
Disruption	no disruption	minor disruption	moderate disruption	complete disruption
	1	2	3	4
Gains	all gains	large gains	modest gains	no gains
	1	2	3	4

Losses	no losses	modest losses	large losses	all losses
	1	2	3	4

Interpreting your scores

Add your scores for each of the seven factors. The total score will be between 7 and 28. Compare your total score with the scales shown below.

Score	Interpretation
Score 1–9	**Short transition period** This level of score shows that you should be able to manage your change fairly easily as most of the factors will not have an adverse effect on you. If you have scored over 7 you will have to consider one or two of the factors and manage more carefully. You should plan how to do so by completing the action plan in the next section.
Score 10–19	**Medium transition period** This level of score shows that you must think carefully about the higher scoring transition factors. One or several factors will have to be carefully analysed and managed. Plan how you will do this in the next section.
Score 20–28	**Long transition period** A score within this range shows that most of the transition factors will disrupt you and prolong your transition period. You will have to spend a great deal of your time coming to terms with the change and developing approaches for overcoming its effects. Examine the factors to which you allocated the maximum four points. Make sure that you develop workable plans to overcome these factors using the action plan in the next section.

Plotting your transition route

You will now have more thoughts on the length of your transition period and the way it can be managed. To help you do this plot a transition route as shown in Figure 9.1. Mark your transition score on the left-hand side of the diagram. Estimate the length of time you think it will take you to overcome the change by referring to the figures on the bottom of the diagram. Connect the two points with a line as shown by the example. This is your transition route from the old to the new. It has to be understood and carefully managed.

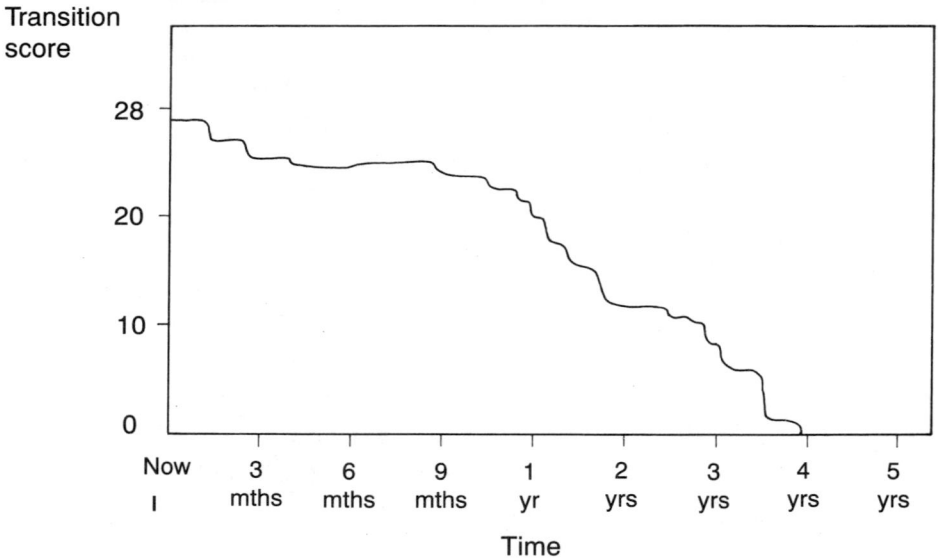

Figure 9.1   Transition route

Your action plan

Consider your score on Exercise 9.2 and reflect upon the length of your transition period. Think of ways to make your transition period shorter, less stressful and disruptive. Use the transition factors in Exercise 9.2 to help you. Concentrate on those with a high score of 3 or 4. It is these factors that must be managed and their effects on you reduced. If necessary refer to the sections that you have completed. In particular reflect upon the spot checks at the end of each section as these will hold valuable clues for reducing the length of your transition period. Write down your proposed actions below.

My action plan

Spot check

Now that you have completed Section 9 write down the three most important points you have learned about adapting to change.

My learning
1
2
3

10 Resilience rebuilds itself

Don't compromise yourself
You are all you've got.
Janis Joplin

Section 9 shows that it takes time to move from one set of circumstances to another when that move is brought on by fundamental change. Few people are able to change rapidly. They have to go through a lengthy process in the course of which they frequently suffer stress and pain, which can strip them of their strength, confidence and resilience and make them vulnerable. If the change is managed correctly the original resilience will return and, furthermore, it will be increased by the experience. Thus the individual grows stronger and is better able to cope with further change.

The process
When a person is subjected to radical change they undergo a process that affects them physically, psychologically and materially. This process is illustrated in Figure 10.1.

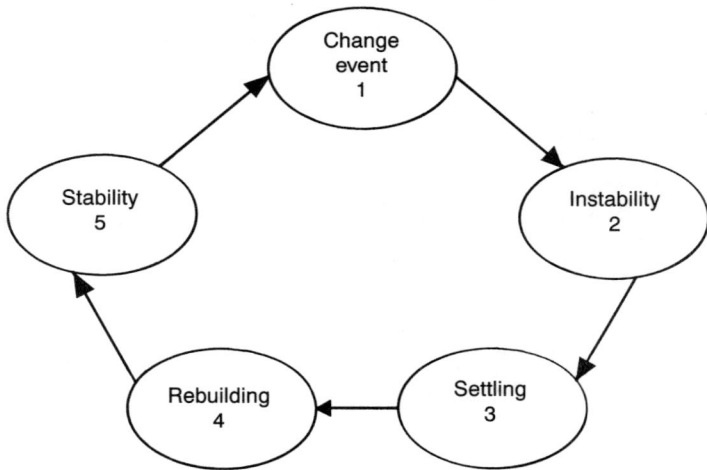

Figure 10.1   Instability/stability process

The stages

Stage 1   Change event
A person has been living a relatively stable life or at least a life that is under control. A new event suddenly affects them. This may be redundancy, divorce, bereavement, business failure and so on. The change event leads to the instability of Stage 2.

Stage 2   Instability
The change produces a state of instability and a loss of equilibrium. The instability may be material. For example, a person loses their job and is unable to pay the mortgage on their house. The property is repossessed by the building society.

The instability may be psychological. A person loses their partner in a car accident. This causes them to have a nervous breakdown and makes them incapable of working and leading a normal life.

The instability may be physical. For example, a person has a heart attack which prevents them from living their normal life and continuing with their previous strenuous occupation and interests.

Some changes may involve two or all three of these instability factors.

Stage 3 Settling

Being in a state of instability is uncomfortable and stressful for most people. They seek to eliminate or reduce the factors in their lives that are causing anxiety or distress and build on those that will be their future. Stage 3 is often a very difficult time as a person may have invested a considerable amount of time, energy, emotion and resources in the past, which may now have to be abandoned. A person may be in an uncertain state for a considerable time, torn between a past which is slipping away and an unknown future. In this period strong feelings and emotions may dominate a person's life. However, a person will eventually begin to take a balanced view of their life as emotions subside and they are able to take a more detached approach. They rely upon their emotions for support as discussed in Section 8 and slowly build. Certain aspects of their situation become more important and firmer ground develops in their lives.

Stage 4 Rebuilding

Some of the initiatives and decisions taken during the Settling Stage may turn out to be wrong or inappropriate. A person who is divorced may start another relationship and find that it was entered into too hastily. A redundant bank manager who sets up as a financial consultant dislikes selling and working in the evenings. Before stability is achieved a person may have to experiment with a number of options. Eventually certain options are accepted and new directions set and worked at. The uncertainty and strong feelings that were brought on by the change are dissipated. The divorcee settles down in a new home with a new partner. The redundant bank manager finds a job with another financial institution although at a lower grade.

Life is now starting to become more predictable with worry and uncertainty removed.

Stage 5   Stability

The crisis is over, survival has been achieved and plans can once again be made for the future. These decisions are made from a position of strength and confidence rather than the weakness of earlier times. A direction has been set and the individual builds factors to achieve their goals. A person who was made redundant has secured another position. They are performing well and looking for further recognition and success. The person who has undergone a traumatic divorce and the breakup of their home and family life has settled into another stable relationship. They feel happy and secure with their new partner and surroundings, having accepted their changed circumstances and adapted to them.

Reaching equilibrium

Every change brings both losses and gains to the person undergoing it. To manage the change successfully it is important that the gains are greater than the losses. It may seem impossible to convince a person who has lost their job and had their house repossessed that the change has brought them more gains than losses, but they must eventually reach this conclusion if they are to accept their changed circumstances and not become permanently angry, resentful or depressed. Some of the losses that can result from a change are described below.

Standard of living

A change of circumstances can drastically alter a person's living standards. If a family's or a person's income is curtailed or restricted they may have to change their lifestyle completely. They may have to give up the overseas holidays, the comfortable house and the car because the income has stopped through job loss, divorce, business failure or a breakdown of relationships. The drop in standard of living may not be as drastic as this but nevertheless it can be painful and difficult to come to terms with.

Material possessions

Along with a loss of income there may also be a loss of material possessions. Items such as the car, caravan and smart clothes may have to be sacrificed. For some people, possessions are symbols that show to the outside world a person's position and standing. For other people, material possessions bring a feeling of satisfaction and achievement, making them feel good as they wear them, have contact with them and use them. Losing their possessions may cause people to lose part of themselves and create a void in their lives.

Status

When adverse change affects a person they may lose status. For example, an individual in a well paid and prestigious job may be an official of several clubs and societies. If they lose their job and are unable to find one of equivalent standing they may also have to resign official posts that are dependent on a person's job.

Loss of income can also result in a lowering of status. The person may no longer be able to afford a subscription to the music society, theatre or sports club.

Self-image

A person's self-image is often related to their job, their successes, the quality of their relationships and their assessment of how effectively they achieve their goals. In a period of adverse change, self-image can be seriously damaged. An individual may lose confidence and mistrust their judgement. Decisions or actions that they previously handled with confidence become difficult to deal with.

In the rebuilding process, losses always result in gains provided the loss is carefully managed and perceived in a correct and positive manner. The successful change manager turns the loss into a gain. There is no choice if a person is to forget the past and start afresh. The longer they hold on to the past the more it will drag them down and prevent them from starting something new and rebuilding their resilience. Some of the gains from a radical change are described below.

A change of direction

An event that dramatically transforms a person's life can be the catalyst for a change of direction. Too often a person is carried along by the circumstances in their life. They allow themselves to be driven by their job, their careers, their relationships and make little attempt to take control of themselves and the direction in which they are heading. Sometimes the kind of life that they are leading and the effect that it is having on them can be detrimental and a danger to their long-term health and well-being. One person may be in a relationship that causes great unhappiness. Another person may be in a job with long and unsociable hours that makes them tired and stressed. A third person could have crippling financial responsibilities that make them a prisoner of a bank and a financial institution. The commitment to paying off their debts restricts their lifestyle and prevents them from experiencing the pleasures of holidays, eating out and so on. When radical change affects people in these kinds of lifestyle, they may see the paucity of their existence and abandon their lifestyle for something more conducive to their temperaments and desires. Sometimes the change directly forces a change in lifestyle, for example the person whose job was too demanding and stressful becomes redundant. She has to find another job and settles for one more suited to her ability and temperament. Similarly individuals who are financially over-committed may lose their home because they are unable to keep up with their mortgage repayments. This shock makes them recognize the impracticality of their lifestyle and they rearrange their finances to better suit their circumstances.

New ways of thinking

The pause in a person's lifestyle after they have been affected by profound change, may lead not only to a new direction but also to a different way of thinking. A thrusting, acquisitive business person may become bankrupt causing them to question their values and the ethos by which they have lived their life. They may start to appreciate the more spiritual and aesthetic aspects of their environment and divert part of their energy from the capitalist endeavour to the pursuit of religious understanding. They may join their local church and become a member of the choir.

A change of thinking can occur in any part of a person's life. Many people change their political affiliation when they have been affected by an event that they see as being part of a political party's policy. Thus the father of a handicapped baby may change his politics and support the political party that he perceives as doing more for the needs of his child.

Time to evaluate
The void that is left when a person is shaken by far-reaching change is an ideal time to evaluate life's circumstances and events. If the change, such as divorce, death, redundancy, business failure, financial hardship and so on, has resulted in the disappearance of large parts of a person's existing life they have several new options on which to rebuild but the transition from one mode of living to another rarely occurs immediately; it is a process and it takes time. In this period of uncertainty a person is able to reflect upon their past life, the quality of their existence, and their general satisfaction and happiness. This reassessment is possible because of the shock of the change, the vacuum it has created and the need to replace that which is lost. The period of reflection and evaluation can be extremely beneficial, especially if a person is able to take control and plan to do what they wish rather than being influenced, cajoled or forced by other people. This evaluation period if used wisely should be one of the principal gains in the process of change. A wise person resets their direction.

Strength
Another important gain to the individual that change brings is a greater personal strength to deal with events that are distress-

ing. After a time of suffering the pain caused by the change, an individual comes to terms with the loss or begins to accept it. The pain dissipates and slowly normality is reached. By going through the change the person learns how to deal with similar situations.

This strength comes from a variety of sources, one of the most important being that the person has conquered a very difficult and traumatic situation. This success confers a higher level of confidence and self-esteem. Another factor is that most people have a natural drive to survive and overcome difficulties. No matter how devastating the change most people will pull through it. Also important is that the change event can often be perceived as being more disruptive and devastating than it actually turns out. A person learns that their first feelings and thoughts can be negatively overstated. The reality is not as bad as they at first think.

Some people develop a greater strength by re-adjusting their values of what is important in their life. A person who has relentlessly pursued status and power may lose their job and high position. They then go through a period of re-evaluation and begin to appreciate that freedom and personal autonomy make them more content with life. This realization leads to the development of greater assurance and strength.

My resilience

Having read about some of the factors that affect your resilience, consider it in detail and decide if you wish to increase it. Start this process by completing Exercise 10.1.

Exercise 10.1   How I feel

Your feelings are an outward expression of your resilience. Written below are words that describe feelings. Circle those that describe your feelings about the change that you are now facing. Circle as many words or as few words as you wish.

jubilant	unhappy	stable	unhealthy
excited	worried	happy	
scared	satisfied	free	uncertain
restrained	anxious	first class	
subdued	alone	independent	constrained
in control	progressing	weary	
exuberant	worn out	healthy	dull
in a crisis	robust	fragile	
dormant	bright	strong	foolish
dynamic	sparkling	struggling	
calm	resentful	carefree	rejected
second-rate	alert	weak	
together	sick	delighted	jaded
joyful	doubtful	refurbished	stuck

Assessing your resilience

Tick any words that you have circled in the previous section in one of the columns of high resilience feelings or low resilience feelings shown below. Then add the number of ticks for each column to produce a total.

Higher resilience feelings (HRF)	Lower resilience feelings (LRF)
jubilant	unhappy
stable	unhealthy
excited	worried
happy	scared
satisfied	uncertain
free	anxious
restrained	subdued
first class	alone
independent	constrained
in control	weary
progressing	worn out
exuberant	dull
healthy	in a crisis
robust	fragile
bright	dormant
strong	foolish
dynamic	struggling
sparkling	resentful
calm	rejected
carefree	second-rate
alert	weak
together	sick
delighted	jaded
joyful	doubtful
refurbished	stuck
Total	**Total**

Interpretation of your score

The Higher Resilience Feelings (HRF) show a positive and controlled attitude to your change. The higher the score in this column the greater the control of the change. The maximum score is 25 if all the words are ticked, although it is unlikely that you would score so high. A score of 10 to 12 shows very positive resilience feelings.

The Lower Resilience Feelings (LRF) indicate a struggle to cope with the change. The higher the score in this column the greater difficulty you have in dealing with the change. The maximum score is 25 if all the words are ticked.

The scores can be interpreted in the following ways.

Score	Interpretation
HRF score 25–10 LRF score 5–0	High resilience This shows you are in charge of the change. You are coping very well and should continue to develop by further enhancing the HRF and decreasing the LRF.
HRF score 15–5 LRF score 5–10	Medium resilience This shows you are coping relatively well with the change and have positive feelings towards it. However, you also have a number of LRFs which are holding back your progress. These need to be examined and worked out.
HRF score 5–0 LRF score 10–25	Low resilience This shows you are having difficulty in coping with the change. It may be that the change has only just affected you (as described on page 110 in the Instability/Stability Process). Alternatively the change could be having a detrimental effect on you which you have been unable to manage successfully.

My resilience

Now that you have completed Section 10 and have explored resilience, describe below the actions that you must take to increase your resilience.

Actions to increase my resilience

Spot check

Having completed Section 10 write down the three most important points you have learned about resilience.

My learning
1
2
3

Summary

Some of the personal analysis and exercises that you have completed in Stage II may have seemed strange to you and perhaps at times rather disturbing. The process of introspection (looking into yourself and understanding yourself) is not easy and is a never-ending journey. Yet it is only by understanding your feelings and managing yourself that you will be able successfully to negotiate your changing environment.

How clearly do you understand the effects of stress on your physical and mental well-being and are you doing sufficient to alleviate it? Stress management like change management is a continuous process which has to be worked at.

As you manage your change keep a check on your resilience score (Exercise 10.1 How I feel). You will find that the score will increase as you regain control and begin to direct events.

STAGE III
Moving on

Introduction

Radical change often destroys some or much of a person's lifestyle or environment. At the same time as working on yourself as highlighted in Stage II you also have to adapt to and create a new vision and goals for the rest of your life. Before this can be done existing paradigms have to be discarded and replaced by ones appropriate to your new circumstances.

The abandonment of old paradigms is not an easy task as it may involve disposing of cherished and long-held beliefs, values, expectations and goals. Most of us try to hold onto old paradigms for as long as possible but there is a point where they have to be replaced as they prevent the new life beginning.

With the adoption of new paradigms comes a clearer direction, an increase in energy and the excitement of creating something different and new. Furthermore you may be able to support others around you who need help in coping with change.

11 New paradigms

It is the eye which makes the horizon.
Emerson

If you are experiencing fundamental change you may have to accept that it will alter you and the way that you live your life. There is no point in attempting to cling to what is past. The change enables you to consider and explore areas that were previously unimaginable. If your change management is to be successful you will need to abandon old paradigms and adopt new ones.

Paradigms

The dictionary definition of a paradigm is a pattern, example or model. In everyday life paradigms are the way that we perceive events or the way that things are arranged. Paradigms influence nearly every aspect of the way we live our lives. It is expected that children will go to school; a person who needs an operation goes into hospital; people will learn about world events through newspapers, radio or television; people will work to earn a living; people will eat fruit and vegetables; football is played on a Saturday. Paradigms bring order into our lives and make life predictable and they are therefore very useful, but there are other important aspects of paradigms that you must also understand if you are to effectively manage change. These are outlined below.

Paradigms slowly change

Life is full of examples of changing paradigms. Over several years one has seen such changes as the movement from meat-eating to vegetarianism, the growth of the word processor and the decline of the typewriter, British families taking holidays abroad, the movement from marriage to relationships, the swing from beer-drinking to the drinking of wines and cock-tails and the pedestrianization of town and city centres. There is almost no aspect of a person's life that is not affected by para-digms that are slowly evolving and changing.

Paradigms can change rapidly

While many paradigms evolve slowly over many years others change rapidly, almost overnight. For example, the breakdown of communism and the pulling down of the Berlin Wall, the decimation of the British coal industry, the collapse of property values and the invention of the quartz watch. These rapid changes often bring turbulence and uncertainty to the lives of the people involved.

Reasons for paradigm changes

The impetus for a change in paradigms can come from many sources. It may be technological invention as in the case of the word processor or the quartz watch. Economic and commercial factors directly influenced the decline of the property market; economic and political forces prompted the demise of commu-nism in Russia. The growth of vegetarianism and the change to more pure and organically grown foods are related to increased public awareness of and concern about the treatment of animals and the use of chemicals in food production.

Different levels of paradigms

Paradigms occur at all levels of our thinking from global, international, national and regional to family and individual. Many of these paradigms we may find interesting but not particularly relevant to us as they have no impact on our everyday lives. You may have watched on television the breakdown of the communist paradigm as the Berlin Wall was dismantled. Perhaps you found it exciting but you felt safe as your life would not be affected. However, you may feel threatened if told that your organization is changing its operational paradigm and plans to introduce advanced computer systems and open plan offices.

Individual paradigms

It is at the individual level that paradigms have the greatest effect on our ability to cope with change. For many people their paradigms are their gateways to the future. The 17 year old who is taking 'A' levels and then expecting to study at university before embarking on a career as a pharmacist has a well-developed paradigm. Also possessing a specific paradigm about the future is the 50-year-old clerk working in local government who anticipates working for another 10 years and then taking early retirement and moving to a bungalow by the seaside.

Paradigm dangers

One of the dangers of paradigms is that they can frequently inhibit the management of personal change. When faced with rapid change we do not accept it and therefore become resistant. We are unable to change our paradigm or incorporate the new idea into our existing paradigm. Any adjustment is made even more difficult as we surround ourselves with 'paradigm reinforcers' – people, information, events and circumstances that maintain the paradigm and help to convince us of its validity.

Examples of paradigms and the way in which they are maintained are discussed in the following case studies.

Joanne's paradigm

Joanne is a 51-year-old personnel officer working for a local authority. The council has to cut its budget by 7 per cent as funding from national government has been reduced. A voluntary redundancy programme has been introduced and anyone over the age of 50 is being encouraged to retire early. Joanne faces a difficult dilemma. She has a great interest in Turkish costume jewellery, which started when she went on holiday to Turkey some 10 years ago. She discovered a small workshop that made a wide range of innovative, well-designed jewellery and on subsequent visits to Turkey she purchased a number of items which she sold to friends and relatives. They also were impressed with the jewellery. On Joanne's last visit to Turkey the owner of the workshop suggested that she set up a business in England selling his jewellery. Such a venture is a possibility now that Joanne can take early retirement but she has a paradigm against small businesses.

One of the reasons that Joanne accepted a position with the local authority was because she regarded it as safe and stable. Her mother and father had run a shop and newsagents and this had dominated their lives and left little time for their children. The business had not been profitable and consequently they were always struggling to make ends meet.

Unlike her childhood, adult life for Joanne had been predictable and routine. She joined the authority at 16 and had worked for it ever since, working part-time while her children were young and resuming full-time work when the youngest was 14.

Joanne's husband Peter was an administrator at the local hospital and all of their friends were drawn from either the local authority or the hospital. Therefore Joanne's paradigm of life was an existence of regular income, order and stability. This paradigm was reinforced by her friends, hobbies and activities. Should she break with her existing ways of thinking and acting and take the financial and personal risk of setting up a small business?

Damien's paradigm

Damien is a young man of 23, working as a labourer in a builders' merchant's yard. People come to the yard to buy bricks, tiles, sand, cement, fencing, wood, slabs, garden fixtures and fittings and DIY items for houses and gardens. Customers order and pay for their goods from a central office and then bring an order form to Damien and his workmates who locate the items and load them into the customers' vehicles.

Damien has worked for the firm and done the same job since he left school 10 years ago. His early years at school had been rewarding and promising. He was an intelligent, alert and receptive pupil who was good at sport and showed academic promise. However, at the age of 12 everything started to go wrong. His mother announced that she and his father were divorcing and his father left home. Within a few months another man moved in with the family. Damien was immediately hostile to this arrangement and withdrew from family life, having little relationship with his mother or her partner. He also withdrew from schoolwork. He played truant, was often late, and was disobedient and sometimes aggressive to staff. His interest in sport stopped and his nights and weekends were spent with a small gang who were often disruptive and frequently in trouble.

Damien continued in this mode until he left school and managed to secure a job. This job brought some order and stability into his life. Life improved when he left home at 17 and moved into a house with four other teenagers. He became an avid follower of the local football team and enjoyed clubbing and drinking with his friends. He had several girlfriends but recently he met Caroline, a student nurse, and she is beginning to have an effect on his life. She works long hours and is also studying for examinations in her spare time. Her ambition and dedication are beginning to influence Damien. In the past months he has come to the conclusion that he has wasted his time and just drifted through the past 10 years. He knows he is intelligent and capable of achieving greater things in life. He now has to decide how to change his life and use his latent abilities.

Changing paradigms

The examples of Joanne and Damien show that a paradigm is not some abstract notion that marginally influences your life but is central to the way that you have thought about and lived your life in the past and the way that you will live it in the future. If you want to change a paradigm there are a number of stages that you must go through.

Stage 1   Recognize your existing paradigm

You should be dissatisfied with what your existing paradigm is doing to your life. This dissatisfaction may arise because your paradigm is preventing you from adopting a new way of thinking and behaving. This is Damien's dilemma, he realizes that he must change to lead a more useful and fulfilling life but is uncertain how to do it. Joanne's past is also acting as a barrier to her possible new venture. Would she be able to withstand the insecurity of working in a small business? What if she were to fail and lose money?

Stage 2   Imagine your new paradigm

Allow your mind to freewheel and dream about how your life would be if you were to change completely and adopt the different lifestyle that the new paradigm would bring. This projection can sometimes be difficult because you do not have a complete picture of the future. To help build up this picture it is often useful to adopt another person as a role model. This role model will be someone that you know and who has successfully changed their position and circumstances. Joanne should identify a person who runs a small business and think about their lifestyle and the way in which they live and then decide if such a life would be appropriate to her.

The choice of role model is significant. You can select an unsuccessful and negative role model that will destroy any new paradigms, or you can select a role model who has been successful in managing their change. Such a person would act as a positive influence and motivator. Damien should adopt as a role model someone who has succeeded from similar circumstances to his own. He will then have a much clearer picture of the new paradigm. He will be able to relate to actual examples of the role model's behaviour and lifestyle.

Stage 3   The consequences of not changing

The decision to adopt a new paradigm will be greatly influenced by the view that you have of your future if you do not change. You should assess what your life will be like in say five or ten years. For example, Damien can see that he would be a frustrated and perhaps angry person. Caroline would be busy pursuing her career while he was working in a job that had few prospects and made little use of his talents.

The decision to change or not to change is therefore dependent upon your view of your future. If you are satisfied with what you see it is unlikely that you will adopt a new paradigm.

Stage 4   The loss/gain equation

The final decision on whether or not to change will be based on your assessment of your losses and gains. Joanne, for example, could hold onto her job and not take early retirement. In the future the authority may impose compulsory redundancy and then she would be unemployed. Furthermore she may have lost the chance of starting the jewellery business. She could take early retirement now and be assured of a pension and also the opportunity of importing the Turkish jewellery and starting what she believes will be a very successful business. She has doubts though because of the struggle her parents had with their small business and the long hours they worked. There is also the risk that the business might not succeed which could leave her with considerable debts at a time in her life when money reserves and income are important.

Planning the change

You should now complete the four-stage process for changing your paradigm. Complete each of the stages, following the instructions.

Stage 1   My existing paradigm

Consider the change that you are now facing and describe your existing paradigm in relation to the change. Is your present way of thinking blocking the change and causing you pain and stress? Do you want to change your paradigm to one that is more appropriate to the future conditions in which you will have to exist?

Describe your present situation below.

My existing paradigm

Stage 2   Imagine your new paradigm

Let your mind wander and think about your ideal paradigm for the future. If possible sit back in a comfortable chair, close your eyes and imagine the ideal situation. At first you may entertain thoughts that are pure fantasy. Do not discourage these thoughts as they will aid your free-thinking creative process. Consider the many options that may be open to you. Slowly eliminate those features of your paradigm that are not feasible until you are left with a view that you think can be achieved.

Describe your future paradigm below.

My future paradigm

Stage 3   The consequences of not changing

To check your choices in abandoning the old paradigm and adopting the new paradigm define the consequences of not adopting the new models and patterns of thinking. Some of these consequences will be serious and will have a detrimental effect on you. When you have identified the consequences you should also be convinced that you have made the correct choice.

Detail below the consequences as you see them.

The consequences of not changing

Stage 4   The loss/gain equation

To manage the transition from the old to the new you should be fully aware of the losses that you will incur from the old and the gains to be accrued from the new. The losses and gains may be emotional, physical, status, authority, position, financial and so on. As a test of your decision the gains should be greater than the losses. An overall gain will give you confidence in making the change.

Detail the losses and gains below.

Losses from old paradigm	Gains from new paradigm

Spot check

Now that you have completed Section 11, identify and describe the three most important points you have learned about new paradigms.

My learning
1
2
3

12 Facing the future

One does not discover new lands without consenting to lose sight of the shore for a long time.
André Gide

The breakdown of one paradigm and the gradual development and adoption of another is essential if you are to manage your change successfully. As the paradigm evolves, you develop a view of your future and its components. This view becomes the foundation on which you can build. In this section you develop the view of your future.

The future emerges

Your life is built up of segments of interests, activities, work, relationships, material possessions, personal particulars such as your health, religion and so on. When radical change affects you then one, some, or all of these factors plus the uncertainty about what will replace them can cause pain and distress.

Change can be managed more easily if you have a vision of your future and you are able to accept this future. Sometimes people have to accept and settle for minor changes in their lives. For example, a person who was earning £20 000 per year has overtime and bonus payments stopped and therefore has to

141

now live on £15 000 per year. This drop in income means a reduction in family spending on food, clothes and household items, a curtailing of holidays and a general lowering of the standard of living. The person is forced to accept these changes as the alternative would be the loss of their job which would have had far greater consequences for them and their family. After a time the family learns to live with its changed circumstances and begins to accept them.

Other features can have a far more profound effect on a person. Consider the case of an international sportstar who earns large sums of money, is revered by an adoring public, appears in the media and lives in luxurious surroundings and then has to give up sport, through ill health or injury. In a short time their life could be transformed from celebrity to has-been, from superstar to office worker or sales representative. There is a massive drop in income and standard of living and a new network of friends and relationships may have to be developed.

The successful management of personal change requires you to assess your present position, understand the effects that the change will have on you, describe what your future will be and accept and adapt to your new future. The following exercise will take you through the stages described above.

Exercise 12.1   My future

Stage 1   Elements in my life
This exercise is in four stages. Stage 1 is to identify the elements that make up your life. Think of everything that is in your life and is important to you. A list of some examples is provided below.

family	food	car
children	gardening	neighbourhood
home	music	clothes
mother	friends	environment
father	work	pets
money	education	painting
religion	health	countryside
hobbies	happiness	computers
holidays	sport	wild life

List the main factors in your life in the first column of the exercise sheet on p. 147 adding to the example list as necessary. Arrange the items in order of importance to you: 1 is most important, 2 second most important and so on.

Stage 2   How it is now
Describe each factor as it is now or how it was before the change. Add this in the second column of the exercise sheet. An example is given below of a person who is made redundant from their job. When describing the factors concentrate only on the main features; don't go into too much detail.

Factor	How it is now	How it will change	How I will manage the change
Family finances	I earn £21 000 per year as a retail manager in a superstore. My wife earns £18 000 per year as a probation officer.		
Our home	We have an old detached house which we are gradually renovating. We are buying it on a £55 000 mortgage.		

Stage 3   How it will change

Now describe the way in which each of the factors will change based upon your assessment of the situation. Remember that this is only one scenario; in times of change other events can be triggered which can greatly influence you and your circumstances. Sometimes these other events can drastically change the situation. However, given your present circumstances describe how you see the factors changing. Follow the example of the redundant retail manager as shown below.

Stage 4   How I will manage the change

For each of the factors you are now aware of the current position and the probable situation after the change has taken place. The transition to the new set of circumstances may not be easy, particularly if you are losing a great deal. You must try to control the situation and not let events take control of you. This will not always be easy especially if the change has shocked

Factor	How it is now	How it will change	How I will manage the change
Family finances	I earn £21 000 per year as a retail manager in a superstore. My wife earns £18 000 per year as a probation officer.	I will have difficulty finding a similar job at my age of 52 years. I may have to settle for a job paying £10 000 per year. I will get some work!	
Our home	We have an old detached house which we are gradually renovating. We are buying it on a £55 000 mortgage.	With my redundancy pay and drastic reduction in our spending we will be able to pay the £350 a month mortgage. The house should be safe for the next year.	

and unnerved you and you are feeling emotional and stressed. Try to think rationally about what must be done and record your outline plans in the column headed, 'How I will manage the change'. The example continues below.

Factor	How it is now	How it will change	How I will manage the change
Family finances	I earn £21 000 per year as a retail manager in a superstore. My wife earns £18 000 per year as a probation officer.	I will have difficulty finding a similar job at my age of 52 years. I may have to settle for a job paying £10 000 per year. I will get some work!	I will be positive and active in seeking a job. I will put as much time, effort and energy into finding another job as I have put into my last job. Methods to be used are a) join a job club, b) personal contacts, c) enrol with agencies, d) reply to adverts. I will aim initially for a similar job but then aim lower if I'm unsuccessful.
Our home	We have an old detached house which we are gradually renovating. We are buying it on a £55 000 mortgage	With my redundancy pay and drastic reduction in our spending we will be able to pay the £350 a month mortgage. The house should be safe for the next year.	Discuss immediately with wife and family methods of reducing expenditure. Areas to consider are a) household goods/ services, b) holidays, c) cars, d) entertaining, e) clothes, f) house renovation. If there is no job within 9 months then more drastic measures will have to be considered.

Factors list			
Factor	How it is now	How it will change	How I will manage the change

Factors list continued			
Factor	How it is now	How it will change	How I will manage the change

Factors list continued			
Factor	How it is now	How it will change	How I will manage the change

Change Factors

After completing Exercise 12.1 you now have a much clearer idea of the way that the change will affect you. Remember that the change from one state to another state is never easy, particularly if it means the loss of things that were important to you. There are a number of factors relating to the change that you will need to understand and carefully manage. These are described below.

Forget the past

We often attempt to hold on to elements of the past, which prevents us from making the transition to the new state. Until we accept that events have changed and will never be the same again, we will not come to terms with the new conditions in our life. An example of this is the person who has suffered the breakdown of a close relationship with another person. If they were not responsible for ending the relationship they may be unable to forget and rid themselves of the emotional attachment. Thus they are prevented from forming new relationships with other people. Sometimes this will happen because the person subconsciously refuses to accept that the relationship is over and expects the other person to come back into their life.

A similar state can occur with a person who is demoted and accepts a lower status job in an organization. This change leaves them angry and bitter. They never accept the change and stabilize their emotions. They generate stress for themselves and often perform below standard. It would be far healthier to accept the change and then make plans to regain the lost position and status.

Be positive

Irrespective of the losses that you have incurred your new venture is now your future. Therefore try to maintain a positive attitude and approach everything that you do with enthusiasm. By being positive you will show to others that you are able to overcome difficulties and they will support you and will want to be involved in your activities. A positive attitude also creates energy in yourself and others which will be translated into hard work and a determination to succeed.

The development of a positive attitude results from your own positive thinking. You have to concentrate on the good points of your new situation. Think about the benefits to be gained. Few changes are all losses. But benefits do not always immediately present themselves, they have to be sought. Often benefits gradually emerge after a period of reflection and through discussions with other people. You begin to see different perspectives as time passes.

Time is important. It is unlikely that benefits will be apparent immediately you are demoted or lose your job or have your house repossessed. In time you will establish an equilibrium and you can then start looking for benefits. You will develop a forward looking strategy and cultivate a position attitude.

Involve others

There are few people who can overcome radical change alone. Most people require others to give them help and advice. This support may be just friendly advice or intense counselling. Discussing a situation often leads to a fuller understanding of it and the development of a solution.

Future plans should also include other people. People will be affected by the change affecting you and they are likely to be involved in the solutions that you are proposing. These solutions will be more successful if those people are actively involved and are part of the solutions. The manager who takes redundancy and decides to set up a small business working from home must have the active support of their partner and family. If the family is hostile to the plans and resents turning the family home into business premises then this lack of cooperation will be a substantial obstacle to future success.

Check the direction

Once a new direction has been agreed it should be pursued with vigour and determination – and also sensitivity. You will be entering uncharted territory and irrespective of your desire to succeed you should not press blindly forward. Ideas and plans must be carefully evaluated because there will be many pitfalls to overcome. Some plans may have to be modified as you learn more about your new future. You may have to abandon your goals as it becomes increasing obvious that what you initially thought was a viable proposition is likely to fail. An example of this is the person who has spent 25 years in a large organization and then decides to start their own small business. They want to turn their hobby of collecting antique maps or manufacturing children's toys into a business. These ventures must be entered into with great caution. Products, markets, profitability, resources, commitment and the whole range of factors that influence success and failure should be evaluated. While many people who leave organizations and become self-employed are successful, there are others who lose everything because they have been driven forward by an uncommercial business idea or fail because they have made the wrong decision.

Ensure that you set time aside to review your direction. Involve all the other people who are associated with you in this process. The review will provide an objective evaluation of your present position and will enable you to make decisions about your future.

Resources

Resources must be carefully managed in change situations. Change results in the disruption of a person's job, their home life, their income and standard of living. A person who divorces or breaks up with their partner may have to finance a new home of their own while paying maintenance for the upkeep of their children. A person who loses their job may also lose their income and all the resources they took for granted while in employment. The loss of the company car can temporarily severely limit mobility and lack of access to a fax machine, word processor or photocopier can cause difficulties.

There is also a call on resources to begin the new life. A person may have to borrow money from a bank or remortgage their house to finance their venture. The individual starting their own business will have to invest in office and computer equipment and possibly take a lease on suitable premises.

It takes time

The change from one state to another is rarely quickly achieved. There are usually many stages to go through and obstacles to be overcome. When planning your change programme you should set a *realistic* time limit for completion – weeks, months or years. Where changes require a long time frame, the stages of the process should be timed. These timings will give you targets to aim at and will also ensure that you maintain your motivation and energy. For example, if you are redundant and seeking another job you should set targets for the number of applications that you submit, the number of interviews that you attend and a target date for obtaining a job. You should take into account the factors that will affect your job applications such as your age, the current economic situation and the level of unemployment. These factors will greatly influence the time taken to obtain employment.

Celebrate successes

The transition from one situation to another can be a long and tortuous process. Disappointments may occur which will make you feel deflated or depressed but you will also have successes as you achieve goals and objectives. Celebrate these achievements by rewarding yourself and other people who have contributed. Treat yourself to a present, take your family or friends to a show or arrange a meal in your favourite restaurant. Ensure that the successes are recognized as important stages in achieving your ultimate goal. These celebrations will contribute to your energy and motivation and help you to overcome the more difficult parts of the change. The successes will also ensure that you maintain a balanced and positive attitude and you do not develop a negative attitude which will divert your motivation and energy.

The seven factors described above must be carefully managed for you to change successfully. Consider them in greater depth by completing Exercise 12.2.

Exercise 12.2   Change factors

Read again the description of each of the seven factors and decide those that will be important to you and will require your attention. Write alongside each factor actions that you will take to ensure that you manage it correctly.

Factor	How I will manage the factor
Forget the past	
Be positive	
Involve others	
Check the direction	

Factor	How I will manage the factor
Resources	
It takes time	
Celebrate successes	

Spot check

Now that you have completed Section 12, identify and describe the three most important points you have learned about facing the future.

My learning
1
2
3

13 Developing strength

Character building begins in our infancy and continues until death.
Eleanor Roosevelt

Most people will have to deal with change throughout their lives. It is vital to know the techniques and strategies for managing change and you have been learning these in the previous sections. Underlying the effectiveness of all these techniques is your psychological and emotional strength. If you are strong you will have the ability to cope with the most difficult and stressful change. In this section we will explore personal strength and consider means of increasing your strength.

Understanding strength and maturity

An individual develops and grows in many ways. Everyone is aware of their growth to physical maturity and the changes that they undergo in the transition from baby to child, teenager to adult. We also grow intellectually through the process of learning and education. We learn how to read and write and then develop more advanced thinking skills and abilities that enable us to operate computers, appreciate poetry and write reports. A

157

person develops and matures in many areas of human experience as we talk about artistic, spiritual, aesthetic, intellectual and physical maturity. An individual can do little to influence the growth of their physical maturity as we are programmed by our genetic make-up. We all follow the same route from birth to death but we are able to influence our physical state by the kind of lifestyle that we lead. A person who eats correctly, takes regular exercises and generally keeps their body in good shape may live 15 years longer than the person who abuses their health.

Emotional and psychological maturity are influential in being able to cope with change. A person who is emotionally and psychologically mature will be able to manage change more easily than a person with less emotional and psychological strength. They will have the resistance to withstand the pressures that change can bring while at the same time being able to maintain a direction that points to a new future. No matter how severe the events to which they have been subjected they will manage to regain control, reach an equilibrium, accept that the changes have occurred and then set out on a route of optimism and hope.

A person with less emotional and psychological strength and maturity will take longer to recover from the shock and effects of the change. They will be in a state of uncertainty for longer and may have difficulty abandoning the old and forging themselves a new future.

As with most aspects of human characteristics and ability it is possible to grow and develop emotional and psychological maturity, enabling future changes to be handled in a more rational manner and with a positive and successful outcome.

The remainder of this section suggests ideas and techniques for increasing your strength. First complete the questionnaire that indicates your present level.

Exercise 13.1   My strength

The following list of statements shows your psychological and emotional strength. Read each statement and score it from 1 to 5 according to the scheme below:

1 – never true
2 – rarely true
3 – sometimes true
4 – almost always true
5 – always true

Factor	Score
1. I am in control of my life.	
2. I have the strength to deal with any crisis that may occur in my life.	
3. When my plans go wrong I am able to adjust them.	
4. I do not suffer from undue anxiety and stress.	
5. I feel contented with what I have achieved so far in life.	
6. I have clear plans for my life which I am following.	
7. I have a balanced life with several different interests.	
8. If I lost all of my money and possessions I would be able to cope and rebuild my life.	
9. I have family and friends who I can turn to in a crisis.	
10. I have strong values and beliefs which are my foundations of life.	
11. I keep myself physically fit.	
12. I am continually embracing new ideas and learning new things.	
13. I am a strong and resilient person.	

Understanding your scores

The questionnaire comprises 13 factors that contribute to personal strength and maturity. The factors on which you have scored 1, 2 or 3 are particularly relevant to you. These factors are weakening your strength and maturity and you should plan to improve on them. Turn to the next page for a description of the factors.

Psychological and emotional strength

Factor 1   Control of life

Make certain that you are controlling your life and that you are not pushed into situations by other people or circumstances. There are few of us who are able to control our lives totally and have everything that we desire. We have to live with other people and are subjected to continually changing circumstances. The strong and mature person is able to understand the pressures and forces to which they are subjected. This knowledge allows them to set a direction and goals for themselves, which are followed with strength and determination.

Factor 2   Strength to deal with any crisis

A strong and mature person has the confidence to know that they will be able to cope with any crisis. Their confidence may be based on the successful handling of past crises or could be part of their psychological make-up. They know that they are a survivor of life and are able to handle anything that is thrown at them.

Factor 3   Re-adjustment of plans

In periods of rapid change you must be able to cope with the frustration and sometimes distress of complete changes of direction and the abandoning of plans. For example, a person has lost their job and they decide to buy a small business. The prospect of owning and running the business helps them overcome the job loss and they put all their energies and resources into the new venture. At the last moment the owner of the business withdraws the sale and the person is left in limbo – no job, nothing to do and months of valuable time and scarce resources lost. As the saying goes: 'When one door closes another bangs shut in your face.'

The strong, mature person must possess the resilience to overcome such setbacks, seek new opportunities and progress.

Factor 4   Anxiety and stress

Too much worry and stress can be detrimental when dealing with a crisis or rapid change. Your ability to assess a situation objectively and then to make reasoned decisions is weakened. High levels of stress can also reduce your motivation and energy levels. You become lethargic and depressed and lose the desire to fight to overcome your adversity. Moderate levels of stress and anxiety are a positive influence. They create alertness and attentiveness.

Factor 5   Life achievements

Your achievements are a solid foundation which give you psychological strength in periods of rapid change and uncertainty. The achievements will be personal and every person will have different achievements. For example, one person may rate their greatest achievements as learning to swim, playing football for their county and qualifying as a structural engineer. Another person may note their achievements as gaining a degree, qualifying as an architect and becoming a mother. Achievements are important in periods of uncertainty when you may have doubts about your abilities and competence. They remind you of your strengths and the qualities that you possess and the way in which you used them to overcome obstacles in your achievements.

Factor 6   Clear goals and plans

Some people drift through life aimlessly and are pushed around by other people and circumstances. They show little control over their direction and are often ill-prepared to cope with the situations in which they find themselves. Personal strength can be derived from taking the opposite approach – establishing a direction and formulating plans for achieving your goals. Few people's plans cover their entire life, but plans that give a direction to the next few years or even months are very useful. Goals and plans provide a thinking structure and framework for the future which add to your stability. Rapid change and new circumstances may force you to re-adjust your goals and modify plans. The new plans will then give a structure to your activities in the future.

Factor 7   Balanced life

It is preferable to have several priorities and interests in your life. One main priority such as your job, your career or your family puts you in a vulnerable position if it were to suddenly disappear. Life itself would disappear and you would be pitched into a vacuum. It is wise to have several focuses and interests, perhaps your job, partner, children, a hobby, friends and so on. These diverse interests will ensure that you do not develop a biased and distorted view of one area, if that area is causing you pain and distress.

Factor 8   Loss of money and possessions

The loss of all their money and possessions would be a devastating blow to most people. Indeed, it has happened to many people in harsh economic times as their businesses fail, they lose their jobs and they are bankrupted. Overnight a person can lose everything that they have striven for in the last 10, 20 or even 30 years. The people affected are heartbroken and their strength, resilience and maturity are tested to the limit. Life, however, has to continue and be rebuilt. With strength you can see opportunity in such an adversity and you can slowly begin to start anew.

Factor 9   Family and friends

In a crisis your family and friends can be a source of great strength. You have people to talk to who will share your concerns and offer you advice. If the crisis is severe you may be shocked and for a period unable to live a balanced life. Family and friends will be able to look after you and give support.

The change that you are experiencing may deflate your financial resources and it is people who are close to you who are most likely to offer help until you are able to recover.

Perhaps one of the greatest benefits of having a network of sympathetic people around is that you do not feel isolated and have people to call upon if necessary. This knowledge gives you added strength to confront and manage your problems.

Factor 10   Strong values and beliefs

When experiencing profound change in significant areas of your life, strong values and beliefs can be of immense help in managing the change. For example, strong religious or personal beliefs are a foundation on to which you can build. They remain a stable part of you when many areas of your life appear to be slipping away or disintegrating.

There can also be negative aspects to holding strong beliefs and values and this is when the change directly challenges the value. For example, you may value personal honesty and integrity and then find that a close friend has badly let you down. This betrayal may cause you great distress and add to your stress and anxiety. With time you will be able to overcome this failure and re-establish your belief.

Factor 11   Physical fitness

Prolonged periods of personal change can be physically and emotionally taxing. You may be anxious, stressed, sleeping irregularly and unable to eat a balanced diet, which can lead to a deterioration in your physical health, making it more difficult to cope with the psychological effects of the change. If you are facing a stressful and uncomfortable change it may become the centre of your life and you may neglect other important areas as you strive to manage it. You may drink too much, start smoking, stop taking exercise and generally let your health deteriorate. This neglect will add to your difficulties as you become more susceptible to colds and illnesses which reduce your strength and energy. Therefore when attempting to manage difficult and stressful change you should start a strict regime of physical fitness. You will then be able to cope more effectively with the stress and pressures and you will also have another focus in your life. The new emphasis will divert some of the energy away from your problems where it would have been wasted on stress and worry.

Factor 12   New ideas and new learning

An important component of your personal strength is to be continually learning. With the pressures of modern living it is easy to stagnate, to ignore new ideas and to quietly slip into a backwater. You are left behind and feel vulnerable and even scared because you do not understand your changing environment. You begin to lose control as new techniques and technology take over. You should be alert to the new ideas and techniques being introduced into your working environment and life and ensure that you learn about them. Some techniques and computer systems are complex and take a long time to learn, but you must make this personal investment otherwise you will fall behind and feel vulnerable. The environment in which you live is forever changing. You will have strength and confidence if you understand it.

Factor 13   Strong and resilient person

A primary factor contributing to your strength is the personal belief that you are strong and resilient. You know that you will survive the most difficult and painful hardships and emerge successful. Survival does not mean that you have lost nothing. Although your life may have been transformed by the change that has occurred you have settled for the best deal that you could get and have come to terms with it. The transition may have been painful but you have endured it. Indeed the experience has enriched you to the extent that you feel that you could deal with any future catastrophe.

Some people initially know that they are strong and resilient; many others have to experience difficulty and trauma before it is proved to them.

Improving your strength

Having considered the factors that contribute to your personal strength and resilience you should decide if your strength can be improved and then plan to achieve it.

Reflect on each of the 13 factors and also your scores on the questionnaire and decide if you should improve the factor by completing the exercise below.

Factor	Improvement required Yes (✓) No (✓)		Actions to be taken
1 Control of life			
2 Strength to deal with any crisis			
3 Re-adjustment of plans			
4 Anxiety and stress			

Factor	Improvement required Yes (✓) No (✓)		Actions to be taken
5 Life achievements			
6 Clear goals and plans			
7 Balanced life			
8 Loss of money and possessions			
9 Family and friends			

Factor	Improvement required Yes (✓) No (✓)		Actions to be taken
10 Strong values and beliefs			
11 Physical fitness			
12 New ideas and new learning			
13 Strong and resilient person			

Spot check

Now that you have completed Section 13, identify and describe the three most important points you have learned about your strength and resilience.

My learning
1
2
3

14 Helping others

First he wrought and afterwards he taught.
Chaucer

If you are experiencing extreme change there will be other people around you who are also undergoing similar change. In completing the sections in this book you will have gained many insights and a much deeper understanding of the management of personal change. You should therefore help other people to manage their change. This section details how to help others and what you will gain from it.

Helping others helps you

You probably learn more about a subject when you have to teach it than learning by any other method. This is because learning information by rote is of little value when you have to pass it on and explain it to another person. To pass on information effectively you must believe in and fully understand what you are teaching. The teaching process also makes the teacher evaluate and question what they are passing to the learner. The learner may probe and question as they mentally struggle to make sense of ideas and concepts and fit them to their own circumstances. By teaching others you also help yourself manage your own change. As the relationship continues the teacher/learner roles diminish and a mutually supportive relationship develops.

Starting to help others

You must first ensure that you are able to help another person. Have you overcome or have under control any shock, trauma or great stress that was associated with your change? Are you in control of your own change management having a clear direction and plans to follow? Do you have adequate energy and stamina to understand another person's problems and difficulties? Have you sufficient time to spend discussing, coaching and counselling another person? Do you really want to help another person manage their change?

If you decide to proceed there are several points that you must consider. These points are discussed below.

Select the person(s)

Identify a person or several people who are undergoing profound change and who you think would benefit from your help. These people should be having difficulty in managing their change. Remember that not all people who are subjected to change are experiencing difficulty. As discussed previously some people can manage their change perfectly adequately either because they initiated the change or because the change is what they desire.

The people that you identify may be friends, family, colleagues or members of your work team. You should choose whether you wish to work with one, two or a group of people. They must, of course, want to work and share their problems with you. Consider also the kinds of change they are having to manage and decide if you have the skills and expertise to help them. It may be that a person is distraught and unable to function normally because of bereavement, divorce, partnership breakup and so on. This person may need medical attention or the help of a professional counsellor and the support services that they can offer.

If you choose to work with one person you will develop a mutually supportive relationship as you discuss and explore the issues that you are facing.

You may work with two people to form a trio, which provides a wider opportunity for new and different perceptions from each person on the others' changes. The atmosphere and dynamics of three people working together will be very different compared with two people. Each person must be given sufficient time to explore and make plans to manage their change with help from the other two people. Your role with the other two people will evolve depending on how far you have progressed with your own change management. You may be a coach and counsellor to them or you may be an equal partner with their perceptions and advice greatly assisting your change process.

You could form a group of about five people, where each person in the group is required to manage their personal change. Your role would be that of a facilitator. You would ensure that each person had time to discuss the change affecting them and what they planned to do. The other members of the group would offer advice and suggestions. As the group concentrates on one person at a time there would be a number of different perspectives expressed and views put forward which would give a wider and deeper understanding of each person's situation. If the group operated effectively a strong and mutually helpful bond would develop between members. They would support each other and help each other to overcome their difficulties. In facilitating the group and explaining in depth each person's change process you would also learn a great deal about the management of your own personal change.

Approaching the people

After selecting the people to help and then deciding if you will work with individual people or a group you must decide how to approach them. Make sure that the people you approach welcome your help and do not see it as interference. For example, they may have stated during casual conversation that they are experiencing difficulty in managing their change and would like some guidance. To examine the skills required to help others manage their change complete Exercise 14.1.

Exercise 14.1   Helping relationship skills

It requires specific skills to help people successfully manage their change. You should assess yourself in respect of these skills before beginning your helping role. Read the definition of the skill and then rate yourself on the scale. Tick the number that corresponds to the level of your skill.

Skill	Low						High
	1	2	3	4	5	6	7
Sympathy To share others' problems and difficulties and show compassion and give comfort.							
Listening To be quiet and attentive to what people say, not missing any important details.							
Perceptive Having deep insights into people and their problems.							
Flexibility To have an open mind to people and their problems and to be able to change with circumstances.							
Objectivity To maintain a detached overview, not being drawn into others' problems and thereby distorting your view.							
Advising To give information, suggestions and recommendations so that individuals can develop a direction and move forward.							

Skill	Low						High
	1	2	3	4	5	6	7
Patience To be able to deal with the uncertainty, frustrations and stress of others as they struggle to cope and come to terms with their change.							
Understanding Not to condemn or rebuke another person for their actions but to appreciate their current circumstances.							
Stamina To see a programme through to the end.							
Reflection To help a person reflect upon their circumstances and decide appropriate actions.							
Communication To communicate clearly face to face with people.							

To show a level of skill capable of helping a person you should be scoring 4, 5, 6 or 7 on the eleven factors. If on any of the factors you score lower, examine your skill and try to improve it before attempting to help anyone.

Helping others to use this book

The first stage in helping others manage their change could be to introduce them to this book. Offer them a copy and explain that it has been written to help people in their situation. Show them the contents of the book and briefly describe the 14 sections. You should now match the characteristics of the person's change with the relevant section in the book so that they can study the section(s) before their next meeting with you. Some people would rather work on the selected relevant section, as this helps them to tackle their immediate problems, than delay by working through some sections that may not be applicable to them.

Ask the individual to describe the change that they are facing and through discussion help them select the sections that they think are relevant. Complete Exercise 14.2 by indicating with a tick those sections that the individual will be studying and note the reasons that they were chosen. If you are helping several people, duplicate this exercise and keep a copy for each person.

Exercise 14.2   Using this book

Name	Studying Yes (✓)	Notes
Stage I Understanding change		
1 Change is inevitable		
2 Everybody experiences change		
3 Change can alter your life		
4 Out of adversity, opportunity		
Stage II Understanding yourself		
5 Feelings		
6 Change and stress		
7 Attitudes to change		
8 Anchors		
9 Transition periods		
10 Resilience rebuilds itself		
Stage III Moving on		
11 New paradigms		
12 Facing the future		
13 Developing strength		
14 Helping others		

Developing the relationships

The next stages of the relationship with the person(s) will have to be handled with flexibility and understanding. Some people will be shocked and take time to reach conclusions about what they should do or the direction that their life should take. You will have to work with them with great sensitivity until they are able to develop plans. This approach may involve just a single step at a time with many meetings taking place over several months. Other people may suffer less distress and confusion. They may immediately accept the change and want to progress to the next stage in their life with the greatest speed. Your relationship with such people will be as coach or mentor helping them to reach their goals by the fastest and most economic route.

At all times draw upon your experiences of managing your own change. Show that you are an example of a person who has successfully managed the transition from one circumstance to another. You will be able to talk about the feelings, apprehensions and uncertainty that you experienced as you came to terms with your change and how you developed new directions and plans for the future. These shared experiences will lead to a common bond developing between you based upon respect and understanding. You will learn from each other.

Ending the relationship

You should end your supportive relationship when both you and the person(s) you are helping feel that they are capable of coping with the change. At this stage they will have come to terms with what has happened and will be pressing ahead with the new. Their doubt and uncertainty will have diminished and they will have confidence in the future.

Do not maintain the relationship beyond this point at which the person(s) is managing their own change. To do so could result in an unhealthy dependency developing between you, depriving the person of autonomy and self-reliance. If they are keen to explore change management in greater depth they can help others in the same way as you have helped them.

Spot check

Now that you have completed Section 14, identify and describe the three most important points you have learned that will help you to better manage change.

My learning
1
2
3

Summary

Now that you have completed Stage III you should have a much deeper understanding of the change that affected you and its impact on your life and circumstances. You should be viewing your situation from an elevated position with a clear view of the direction to be taken. Other people involved will be enthusiastic and committed as your plans are implemented.

On reflection you may be highly satisfied or even euphoric about how well you have managed change. Think back to your darkest hour and acknowledge how much you have progressed. What were the turning points that led to your progress? How can you further develop your newly found strengths? Remember the remark of Eleanor Roosevelt, 'Character building begins in our infancy and continues until death.' So too does the management of personal change. The more you think about it, study it and practise it the better you will become.

Conclusion

Ask me not where I have travelled or what I have done but what I have learned.
Anon

Every aspect of living is changing: transportation, communication, entertainment, the family, marriage, jobs, computer technology, eating patterns, recreation, health care, shopping, holidays and so on. Over the centuries people have always experienced change. Some have embraced the change while others have resisted it. But never before has the change been so rapid and profound. People adversely affected by change can be left bewildered and shocked and lose direction because they do not have the knowledge, experience, tools and techniques to deal with the change affecting them.

Everything points to an even faster rate of change for the next generations. They should not be left to struggle alone with the effects of change on their lives. People need more frameworks, concepts, tools and assistance to manage change effectively. Over the past years much has been written about the management of change. Change centres have been founded by colleges and universities, consultants specialize in change management and courses proliferate on understanding and managing change. Much has been accomplished but still more needs to be done. Foremost in this work should be an extension of the topic of this book – the effective transition of a person from one situation to another. This transition may appear simple and uncomplicated on the surface but for the person affected it may result in great distress and unhappiness. The reason is that human beings are thinking and emotional entities who are shaped and affected by their living environments. For some people their environment can be their life or at least a substantial part of it. A person made redundant after working for an organization for 25 years may lose not only a source of income but also status in the community, personal identity, friendships, routines, purpose, direction, self-respect, career plans, confidence and so on. Loss of this kind is not easily overcome. Individuals must be aware that attached to each change situation is a reparation time and a reparation rate and they will slowly progress from one position to another. A person filled with resentment, anger or fear will be unable to accept this idea. They live the feelings of the moment and talk of the future will be meaningless to them until they have begun on the pathway of recovery and transition.

An important aspect of personal change management is that the skills and techniques required are not those used every day, such as for communication, language, word processing, car driving, reading or writing. Most people require the skills only when they are being affected by change, which may be once every few years or several times in a lifetime. Thus for the average person to gain a certificate or degree in change management when they are young adults would not be particularly beneficial. A person should be presented with the knowledge and techniques just before they experience change and then given guidance through the process.

The most important tools in the successful management of change are the perceptions, attitudes, skills and resilience of the individual. It is the way that the person handles and manages themselves that determines how well they manage themselves through change. Some people have an inherent capacity to deal with change better than others, based upon their personalities, attributes and skills. But others can learn and build up the necessary qualities in the same way that they can learn computing or management skills. The problem for many people is that they are pitched into change without a script to follow and consequently ad lib their way through a hit and miss performance. This approach is often prolonged through confusion, lack of direction and clarity of aim. Those readers who have used this book as a framework to manage their own change should have learned a great deal from the process. Remember what you have learned because in this rapidly changing world you may need it again – very soon.

Change and the Bottom Line

Alan Warner

A Gower Novel

- How do you plan organizational change?
- How good are you at managing change?
- How do you monitor progress?
- How can you identify resistance - and deal with it?
- What concepts and techniques are available to help?

These are some of the questions addressed in Alan Warner's latest business novel. He takes the characters already established in his two earlier books - *The Bottom Line* and *Beyond the Bottom Line* - and sets them in a new context. Phil Moorley has become CEO of a family firm in the North of England, where his main task is to change its culture so that it can meet the challenges ahead. Once again he enlists the aid of Christine Goodhart, now a training consultant.

We follow Phil's attempts to create allies and pacify enemies, and we share with him the pains and the triumphs involved. We learn about some of the methods that can be used to bring about change and we see how they work - or fail - when put to the test.

Change and the Bottom Line is another highly effective case study, given life by the fictional treatment. An added feature is the detailed commentary provided by the author, drawing on his personal experience of working closely with change specialists. The result is an entertaining introduction to one of the key areas of management responsibility.

Gower

Diary of a Change Agent

Tony Page

Tony Page is a 40-something management consultant, wrestling with the conflicting demands of a growing business and a growing family. For three years he kept a diary to which he confided his hopes and fears, his triumphs and setbacks. With painful honesty he analysed his working and business relationships as he strove to add value to his clients' businesses and to improve his own abilities.

The diary captures a unique personal journey and by including further commentary, analysis and exercises Tony Page both challenges the reader and emphaizes the human component in managing change.

Tony Page's book:

- introduces diary-keeping as a method for continuous professional and personal learning
- demonstrates ways of gaining control over personal performance
- shows how to conduct conversations that empower other people to change and learn
- provides an example and a direction for leaders who want to 'walk the talk'
- uncovers why corporate change programmes fail and how to mobilise people in an organization.

This honest account will have immediate appeal for anyone serious about business performance improvement, change and learning.

Gower

Facilitating Change

Ready-to-Use Training Materials for the Manager

Barry Fletcher

This is a manual designed to help managers to help their staff,
using a range of techniques borrowed from the training
professional's armoury, with full explanation of how any manager
can use them in a team development context. Introductory
chapters describe the principles and methods involved in developing
people to cope confidently with change. There are questionnaires
and suggestions for diagnosing learning needs and recognizing
learning opportunities.

At the heart of the manual is a collection of thirtyfive learning
activities. Each is self-contained but can be combined with others
within the collection to form a more extensive programme of
development. All activities start with a brief description and a note
of potential benefits, guidance over who it is suitable for and the
time and resources required. This is followed by a step-by-step
guide to running the activity. Ready-to-copy masters are supplied
for any material to be used by participants. The activities are
indexed by subject to make it easy for managers to identify the
most appropriate for their own needs.

For any manager who'd like to unlock the full potential of his or
her team, *Facilitating Change* provides an excellent starting point.

Gower

How World Class Companies Became World Class

Studies in Corporate Dynamism

Cuno Pümpin

The globalization of the world economy, unpredictable political developments, dramatic changes in international financial markets, new information technology - to name but a few factors have created a turbulent and rapidly changing business environment. Only dynamic companies will be able to survive under these conditions.

In this innovative book, Cuno Pümpin illustrates how many of the world's most successful corporations have used dynamic principles to increase their market share, multiply their turnover, and unlock value for both shareholders and employees. The author's findings are based on analysis of many successful and dynamic American, European and Japanese corporations. During intensive interviews with top managers, a pattern of how these companies reacted to the challenges of a turbulent environment emerged.

This book focuses on how the dynamic principles practised by these companies have led to their common success, during times when many other companies have failed.

Gower

Managing Through Change

Patricia Wilson

Smart Management Guides Series

In the short, medium and long term there's one thing you can count on in your organization: continuous change. How you cope with this change will determine how successful - and happy - you will be. And it won't be easy. You will need to learn new skills and develop new attitudes.

Managing Through Change outlines these skills and provides a clear, step-by-step approach to help you understand, manage and ultimately facilitate change. Short, punchy chapters and practical checklists help you to anticipate the changes you will face; highlight the advantages of change; take the risk out of change; and help others to deal with change.

Managers and team leaders will find all that they need to build a personal action plan for managing through change.

The Smart Management Guides Series offers practical guidance, with helpful tips and checklists, in a range of essential business skills. With each title providing an instant grounding in a key area, they're ideal for today's busy manager. Other titles in the series include: *Empowering the Self-Directed Team, Unlocking Peak Performance, Managing Your Boss, Essentials of TQM, Assert Yourself, Essential Delegation Skills, Managing Stress, Motivation and Goal Setting* and *Essential Presentation Skills*.

Gower

A Manual for Change

Terry Wilson

Change is now the only constant, as the cliché has it, and organizations who fail to master change are likely to find themselves undone by it.

In this unique manual, Terry Wilson provides the tools for planning and implementing a systematic organizational change programme. The first section enables the user to determine the scope and scale of the programme. Next, a change profile is completed based on twelve key factors. Finally, each of the factors is reviewed in the context of the user's own organization.

Questionnaires and exercises are provided throughout and any manager working through these will have not only a clear understanding of the change process but also specific plans ready to put into action.

Derived from the author's experience of working with organizations at every level and in a wide range of industries, the manual will be invaluable to directors, managers, consultants and professional trainers battling to help their organizations survive and flourish in an increasingly turbulent environment.

Gower

A Real-Life Guide to Organizational Change

George Blair and Sandy Meadows

'Management ideas may change with fashion, but the underlying concepts do not lose their validity. We offer you prepared food for thought for your organizational microwave, rather than exotic dishes that are very difficult to copy.'

George Blair and Sandy Meadows - themselves battle-hardened veterans of the change process - take a refreshingly different approach to most of the new books, videos, seminars and gurus emerging to tell managers how to cope with change. They encourage the reader to start from the reality of his or her own organization and have the courage to design the programme that will work in real life.

Drawing both on proven systems and their own extensive experience, they chart the way forward from strategy to implementation. With the aid of checklists, illustrations and case studies, they show how to diagnose existing problems, how to construct the appropriate plans and how to deal with the politics. They examine the various options, including empowerment, TQM and re-engineering, set out the criteria for selecting the best mix for your own circumstances and then explain the techniques involved in implementation. Unlike many other books on change, they pay due attention to the need for a reward strategy to support the aims of the change programme.

This accessible and often humorous book is firmly grounded in reality, and will be a welcome relief for managers trying to assimilate accepted 'best practice' in change management into their real working lives.

Gower

Takeover

Sam Volard

A Gower Novel

Over the elaborate Christmas festivities at the Human Ethicals Division of AgriBus International falls a shadow in the shape of an alarming rumour. Can it be true that the Division is being sold? And if it is true, what will it mean for the staff of HED? In particular, how will it affect the heroes of Sam Volard's new novel - the assorted but loyal group of friends who we meet in the opening chapters at their traditional Christmas holiday together? Their friendship is about to be put under intense pressure...

For the one-year period covered by the story we follow the reactions of scientists Brian Curtis, Britt Berghoff and Armand Hernier and lawyer Tony Johns, together with their partners and their colleagues. We see how they survive - or fail to survive - the turmoil of redundancies and restructuring until the Division has been fully integrated into the new parent company. At the same time we come to understand the problems of the new divisional chief and his head office team as they deal with the initial trauma and then, with the help of a detailed change model, set about creating a High Involvement Workforce.

Takeover can be read for its fast-moving story and colourful characters. But as we follow the process of the takeover from initial rumour to total integration, we see it from all angles, with good and bad management practice, and all the hopes and fears brought in its wake. The author also provides a chapter-by-chapter commentary analysing the action and underlining the lessons to be drawn. Senior managers will find this a stimulating and rewarding read; one to which many will relate from their own past or current experience.

Gower